1992

The American Novel series provides students of American literature with introductory critical guides to the great works of American literature. Each volume begins with a substantial introduction by a distinguished authority on the text, giving details of the work's composition, publication history, and contemporary reception, as well as a survey of the major critical trends and readings from first publication to the present. This overview is followed by a group of new essays, each specially commissioned from a leading scholar in the field, which together constitute a forum of interpretative methods and prominent contemporary ideas on the text. There are also helpful guides to further reading. Specifically designed for undergraduates, the series will be a powerful resource for anyone engaged in the critical analysis of major American novels and other important texts.

In his introduction to *New Essays on Poe's Major Tales*, Kenneth Silverman sets forth Poe's theory of the tale and examines recurrent motifs in his fiction. The essays that follow present a variety of critical approaches and illuminate different facets of Poe's complex imagination, concentrating on such famous tales as "The Cask of Amontillado," "The Fall of the House of Usher," "The Black Cat," and "The Murders in the Rue Morgue." In interpreting Poe's classic tales, the critics also illuminate such broader issues as his depiction of women, his theory of knowledge, his understanding of perversity, his relation to popular culture, and his preoccupation with death. The essays thus afford a new slant on some longstanding questions in the interpretation of Poe, and frame some new questions raised by current interests in epistemology, psychoanalysis, and cultural studies.

NEW ESSAYS ON POE'S MAJOR TALES

★ THE AMERICAN NOVEL ★

GENERAL EDITOR

Emory Elliott
University of California, Riverside

New Essays on
Poe's Major Tales

Edited by
Kenneth Silverman

CAMBRIDGE
UNIVERSITY PRESS

Published by the Press Syndicate of the University of Cambridge
The Pitt Building, Trumpington Street, Cambridge CB2 1RP
40 West 20th Street, New York, NY 10011-4211, USA
10 Stamford Road, Oakleigh, Victoria 3166, Australia

© Cambridge University Press 1993

First published 1993

Printed in the United States of America

Library of Congress Cataloging-in-Publication Data

New essays on Poe's major tales / edited by Kenneth Silverman.
p. cm. − (The American novel)
Includes bibliographical references (p.   ).
ISBN 0-521-41018-5. − ISBN 0-521-42243-4 (pbk.)
1. Poe, Edgar Allan, 1809–1849 − Fictional works. I. Silverman,
Kenneth. II. Series.
PS2642.F43N48   1993
813'.3 − dc20   92-14571

A catalog record for this book is available from the British Library.

ISBN 0-521-41018-5 hardback
ISBN 0-521-42243-4 paperback

Contents

Contents

5

Poe's Art of Transformation:
"The Cask of Amontillado" in Its Cultural Context
DAVID S. REYNOLDS
page 93

6

Poe, "Ligeia," and the Problem of Dying Women
J. GERALD KENNEDY
page 113

Notes on Contributors
page 131

Selected Bibliography
page 133

Series Editor's Preface

In literary criticism the last twenty-five years have been particularly fruitful. Since the rise of the New Criticism in the 1950s, which focused attention of critics and readers upon the text itself – apart from history, biography, and society – there has emerged a wide variety of critical methods which have brought to literary works a rich diversity of perspectives: social, historical, political, psychological, economic, ideological, and philosophical. While attention to the text itself, as taught by the New Critics, remains at the core of contemporary interpretation, the widely shared assumption that works of art generate many different kinds of interpretations has opened up possibilities for new readings and new meanings.

Before this critical revolution, many works of American literature had come to be taken for granted by earlier generations of readers as having an established set of recognized interpretations. There was a sense among many students that the canon was established and that the larger thematic and interpretative issues had been decided. The task of the new reader was to examine the ways in which elements such as structure, style, and imagery contributed to each novel's acknowledged purpose. But recent criticism has brought these old assumptions into question and has thereby generated a wide variety of original, and often quite surprising, interpretations of the classics, as well as of rediscovered works such as Kate Chopin's *The Awakening*, which has only recently entered the canon of works that scholars and critics study and that teachers assign their students.

The aim of The American Novel Series is to provide students of American literature and culture with introductory critical guides to American novels and other important texts now widely read and studied. Usually devoted to a single work, each volume begins with an introduction by the volume editor, a distinguished authority on the text. The introduction presents details of the work's composition, publication history, and contemporary reception, as well as a survey of the major critical trends and readings from first publication to the present. This overview is followed by four or five original essays, specifically commissioned from senior scholars of established reputation and from outstanding younger critics. Each essay presents a distinct point of view, and together they constitute a forum of interpretative methods and of the best contemporary ideas on each text.

It is our hope that these volumes will convey the vitality of current critical work in American literature, generate new insights and excitement for students of American literature, and inspire new respect for and new perspectives upon these major literary texts.

Emory Elliott
University of California, Riverside

1

Introduction

KENNETH SILVERMAN

The Life of Edgar Allan Poe

MENTION the tales of Edgar Allan Poe, and most readers think at the same time of his life, fusing the two in a single impression of eerie melancholy. The response may seem shallow, but it is not unfounded. Emulating Byron, Poe created through his works a public image of himself as haunted and alienated. Nor was this image unfounded. Poe's experiences were such as to leave him preoccupied with the past and often at odds with his contemporaries' values and ambitions. To explore Poe's tales in the light of his biography is to confirm, with fuller understanding, the popular impression of a single lifework driven by mournful supernaturalism.

Poe's beginnings were traumatic.[1] He was born in Boston on January 19, 1809, the second son of the actors Eliza Poe – a rising star of the American stage – and David Poe, Jr., an incompetent failure who deserted the family when Edgar was about two years old. A year later, his mother, at the age of twenty-four, died during a theatrical tour of the South, probably with her children present.

Orphaned before he was three, Poe was separated from his brother and infant sister, and taken in by a childless Richmond couple, John and Fanny Allan. His upbringing did little to overcome the shocks of his first few years. The couple never formally adopted him and provided rather material comfort than attention and warmth. A prospering Scots merchant, John Allan spoke often of Duty and Obedience and was absorbed in business. Fanny Allan, although an affectionate woman with a capacity for gaiety, was often ill.

1

Poe had his first rigorous education at boarding schools in England, where he accompanied the Allans at the age of six and a half, then at academies in Richmond. Evidencing a gift for languages, he excelled in Latin and began writing verse. Ambitious in other ways as well, he also became known as an outstanding broad jumper, boxer, and especially swimmer.

As he grew into his teens Poe began quarreling more and more heatedly with John Allan, who complained of his behavior as sulky and thankless. His entry to the University of Virginia, early in 1826, brought on a serious rift between them. Again he excelled in his studies, especially in Latin and French. Being about two years younger than the other entering students, however, he found the dissolute atmosphere at the school difficult to manage. After his first year he left the university, owing two thousand dollars or more in gambling and other debts. (He claimed that John Allan had sent him off without enough money to pay his school bills, forcing him to gamble.) Threatened with jail for the debts – which Allan refused to pay – he argued bitterly with his guardian, and in March 1827 left the Allan home. To make his whereabouts uncertain he created a false trail, leading others to believe he had gone to sea or joined the Greek fight for independence. Actually, he had returned to his birthplace, Boston, where in 1827 appeared, anonymously, his first published volume, *Tamerlane and Other Poems.* He also enlisted as a private in the United States Army, under the name "Edgar A. Perry." Again distinguishing himself, he worked his way up to Sergeant Major, the highest possible rank for noncommissioned officers.

The death of Fanny Allan in February 1829, at the age of forty-four, brought about a short-lived reconciliation between Poe and John Allan, who now helped him gain admission to West Point. His efforts to become a commissioned officer were jarred, however, by news of John Allan's remarriage, to a woman twenty years his junior, and by a letter from Allan declaring, as Poe paraphrased it, that his guardian desired "no further communication" with him.[2] Poe replied by contriving to have himself court-martialed. He left West Point, ending his army career.

Exiled from Richmond, Poe settled in Baltimore with the family of his father, the failed actor David Poe, Jr. The impoverished household consisted of his widowed forty-one-year-old aunt, Maria Clemm ("Muddy"), a pious, complaining, overburdened woman, and her nine-year-old daughter, Virginia ("Sissy"). In Baltimore, Poe made his way into professional literary life, writing busily and publishing the first of his acknowledged tales, "Metzengerstein." The period also marked the end of his relation to John Allan, who died in March 1834, leaving an estate estimated at three quarters of a million dollars. The bulk of it he bequeathed to his second wife and the two children he had fathered by her. To Poe he left nothing. Throughout his career Poe struck the Allan name from his own, almost invariably signing himself "Edgar A. Poe."

A chance for the disinherited Poe to earn a dependable income from literature came later the same year when he was offered an editorial post on a new magazine, the Richmond *Southern Literary Messenger*. The income now greatly mattered to him, for he felt obliged to repay Muddy's devotion by supporting his "Mother," as he usually called her. And he had fallen in love with his cousin Sissy and wished to marry her, although she was barely past the age of thirteen. In September 1834 they took out a marriage license in Baltimore, and perhaps were privately married, as they later were publicly. Poe's writing for the *Messenger* generated excitement and gained him his first literary notice, but he fell out with the owner of the magazine and after sixteen months in Richmond, he, Sissy, and Muddy moved to New York City and then to Philadelphia.

Poe's life in Philadelphia over the next six years was marked by an almost continuous struggle to feed himself and his family, by disillusionment with the politics and economic realities of literary life, and apparently by a battle against a need for alcohol. But they were also the most fertile years of his career, first as an assistant editor of *Burton's Gentleman's Magazine* and then as an editor for *Graham's Magazine*, one of the most widely circulated periodicals in America. During this period he wrote such classic tales as "The Fall of the House of Usher," "The Murders in the Rue Morgue," "The Pit and the Pendulum," and "The Gold-Bug." He also laid plans to publish a magazine of his own, "The Stylus," plans he would pursue unsuccessfully the rest of his life. Just the same, Poe barely scratched out a living from his writing. With authorship as a profession just beginning in America, American writers received little for their work. "Ligeia" seems to have earned Poe only ten dollars.

From the results of one particular event in Philadelphia Poe would never recover: around the middle of January 1842, the plump, cherubic Virginia, while singing, began to bleed from her mouth, hemorrhaging in the onset of tuberculosis.

In April 1844, Poe, Sissy, and Muddy settled in New York City. He achieved an entirely new level of celebrity by publishing in a New York newspaper one of the most famous poems ever written. "The Raven" was reprinted at least ten times within a month after its first appearance. While editing a new weekly, *The Broadway Journal,* Poe further increased his fame, or notoriety, by mounting a zealous crusade that came to be known as the "Longfellow War," denouncing the popular New England writer as a plagiarist. At the same time, his worries over the health of Virginia, chronic money problems, and an accumulation of past woes left him depressed, even at times despondent. His erratic behavior estranged his friends, he had difficulty writing, and his flirtation with Frances Sargent Osgood – a well-known poet then nearly thirty-four years old, married, and the mother of two young daughters – turned scandalous, got him into a fist fight, and led to his ostracism from the city's literary salons.

Amid speculation in the press that he had become deranged, Poe and his family left the city around the beginning of March 1846. They moved to a pretty cottage in the rural village of Fordham, about thirteen miles from New York. By now Sissy's condition had badly deteriorated, her complexion had become pearly. Poe, however, brought on another raucous newspaper war by publishing thirty-eight sketches entitled "The Literati of New York City," tartly estimating not only the work of his contemporaries but also their character and physique. The many published counterattacks incited him to bring a suit for libel, which he won. He was in no condition to enjoy the three hundred dollars awarded him, however, for on January 30, 1847, Sissy died of tuberculosis, apparently suffering much pain.

All but undone by the death of his young wife, with its renewed shock of earlier loss, Poe tried frantically to stabilize himself by remarrying. During the summer of 1848, he became more or less involved with three different women. His most likely prospect was the pale, delicate looking poet Sarah Helen Whitman of Providence, Rhode Island, a disciple of Emersonian Transcendentalism. Forty-five years old (his senior by six years) and a widow, she suffered a perhaps imaginary heart ailment that she eased with ether; its odor was said to waft about her. After spending four days with her in Providence, in September 1848, Poe declared his love and proposed marriage. Whitman felt a deep affinity for him, in part based on her occult belief that they were descended from distant branches of the same family. But despite her liberal opinions, she was conservative in her behavior and obedient to her mother, who disapproved of Poe; she told him she needed time to decide. In view of her reluctance, Poe at the same time cultivated a handholding but otherwise Ideal attachment in Lowell, Massachusetts, with a married woman named Annie Richmond, to whom he expressed a willingness to die – for her or with her.

From Lowell, Poe traveled to Providence again in November, feeling conflicted and anxious. By his own account he stopped off in Boston and swallowed an overdose of laudanum in an apparent suicide attempt. He reached Whitman's house three days late for their appointment, and called on her one morning in a state of delirious excitement, pleading with her to save him from doom. Somehow he managed to obtain her consent to what she called a "conditional" engagement. It went as far as announcements in several newspapers that the couple were to be married. But it went no further, being but the halfhearted hope for a marriage that, at bottom, neither party desired.

Poe's final attempt to reestablish a home with Muddy and a new wife came during a visit to Richmond in the summer of 1849. He set out in the possibility of marrying a woman named Elmira Shelton whom he had courted during his adolescence – and also hoping to win subscribers to his ever-elusive "Stylus." But he fell ill and ended up staying almost two weeks in Philadelphia where he apparently began drinking heavily and became, as he described his condition, "totally deranged" for ten days.[3] He believed he overheard some men plotting to kill him and he had tormenting fantasies of his "Mother's" legs being hacked off. Once he reached Richmond he managed to compose himself. Rumors soon circulated that he and Elmira Shelton were to be wed. He bought a wedding ring and, perhaps to impress her with his sobriety, made a public pledge against alcohol by joining a Richmond temperance society.

Poe left Richmond in the early morning of September 27, presumably planning to settle his affairs in New York before returning to Richmond to be married. Nothing is known of his whereabouts over the next week, but on October 3 he was spotted in a Baltimore tavern, raggedly dressed and semiconscious. Taken to a hospital, he reportedly arrived in a stupor but soon began raving at spectral objects. He died at three o'clock on Sunday morning, October 7, 1849, at the age of forty.

Poe's Practice and Theory of the Tale

However messily hectic his personal life, Poe worked at his writing and maintained a strenuous literary career. In addition to editing several magazines, he turned out page after page of trivial journalism, lectured, published a treatise on the origin and destiny of the universe, attempted a play in blank verse (*Politian*), and even gained a reputation as a wizard decoder of cryptograms.

Unlike his major contemporaries, who mostly wrote only fiction (Hawthorne) or poetry (Whitman) or essays (Emerson), Poe was a versatile man of letters who wrote all three. His earlier poems, such as "Dream-Land," "Israfel," and "To Science," exalt the world of dreams and fantasy; his later, more openly autobiographical poems like "To Annie" and the brilliant "Ulalume" brood on such personal disasters as the death of Virginia and his attempted suicide. As a critic, he wrote hundreds of reviews that became notorious for their style of slashing condemnation. Contemporaries often compared him to an American Indian wielding a tomahawk and scalping knife. Poe considered American literary life during his time corrupt. He believed that, through a combination of literary cliques, incompetent editors, and publishers willing to pay for puffs of their books, many mediocre writers became celebrated while some of the most gifted remained unpraised. He used his reviews to right this perceived injustice, relentlessly exposing the deficiencies of the mediocre, and teaching American readers what to appreciate in the best. As a writer of fiction Poe published some seventy tales. He prided himself on their variety. "One of my chief aims," he explained, "has been the widest diversity of subject, thought & especially *tone* and manner of handling."[4] Most were Gothic tales of a kind popular in British magazines of the period, narratives of the marvelous and supernatural such as "The Fall of the House of Usher," involving gloom-ridden aristocratic heroes who inhabit luridly lit moldering mansions. Intended to shock, they are often told by persons who have themselves been traumatized by the events they relate, or whose mental stability is questionable. All convey the presence of an inscrutable, menacing, paranormal world lurking behind the workaday world we know. Poe often fashioned his tales after a popular sub-type of the Gothic known as the Tale of Sensation, in which a victim minutely records his sensations while trapped in some harrowing predicament, as in "The Pit and the Pendulum."

At the other extreme, Poe wrote many broad comic tales, "extravaganzas." "The Angel of the Odd," a typical instance, concerns the freak accidents brought about in human life by a prosthetic angel, a creature made of bottles and kegs who speaks in dialect and has no wings: "Vat I pe do mit te wing? Mein Gott! do you take me vor a shicken?"[5] Although Poe boasted of his sense of humor, such little read works provide no livelier evidence of it than slapstick violence, pedantic verbal play, and weak jokes blown into plots. Not much more wit enlivens his tale-like hoaxes, such as the purportedly factual account he published in a New York newspaper announcing that the Atlantic Ocean had been crossed in three days by balloon. In a still different key are what he described as "*post-mortem* reveries," eerie tales such as "Shadow.—A Fable."[6] In these, departed spirits return to earth or solemnly converse after death about their experiences while passing to the Other Side – his version of the popular visionary fiction of the day that reported scenes and dialogues in heaven. He also wrote several tales of imaginary voyages such as "Hans Phaall," describing the flight of a two-foot tall Dutchman to the moon, and

"The Narrative of Arthur Gordon Pym," his one novella, whose hero faces death by starvation, suffocation, exposure, shipwreck, cannibalism, and worse in his apocalyptic voyage toward the South Pole.

In notable addition to these varied tales of horror, comic violence, otherworldly philosophy, and thrilling adventure, Poe produced what he called his "tales of ratiocination – of profound and searching analysis."[7] Here the keen deductive powers and poetic imagination of the Paris recluse C. Auguste Dupin ponder window latches and folds in paper to unravel the mysteries of "The Murders in the Rue Morgue" or "The Purloined Letter." In these works Poe virtually invented, with little or no precedent, one of the most popular literary entertainments ever conceived, the tale of crime and detection. Many of the devices he introduced remain conventions of the genre even today – the detective's sidekick, the investigation of material clues, the locked-room mystery.

Some reviewers in Poe's time criticized his tales as too "German," too filled with elements of the irrational and supernatural, or thought them obscure, disgusting, or pretentious. (He did sometimes use words and phrases from foreign languages he knew slightly or not at all, such as Spanish and Hebrew.) Overall, however, his tales were highly praised and a few became phenomenally successful. He claimed that his tale of buried treasure, "The Gold-Bug," appeared in more than three hundred thousand copies and was "circulated to a greater extent than any American tale, before or since."[8] He may not have exaggerated, for the often republished work was also made into a play, and became his first tale to be translated, a French version appearing in 1845.

In fact, however criticized for obscurity, Poe meant his fiction to be read. Indeed probably no other writer of the period kept the reader so intently in mind. This is not to say that Poe wrote for "the masses." Rather, he saw no inherent conflict between popular and elite writing. He praised Charles Dickens for confuting the notion "that no work of fiction can fully suit, at the same time, the critical and the popular taste."[9] More than that, he worked out over his lifetime a theory of the tale based on lucid and far-reaching aesthetic principles. It guided his own writing of fiction, which in turn amplified and refined his theory. Anxious to impart standards by which American readers might judge literary works, he set forth his principles here and there in many of his reviews, piecemeal. He also devoted to them two essays that have become classics of American literary criticism. They were occasioned by the one American writer of tales he respected, Nathaniel Hawthorne, whose *Twice-Told Tales* and *Mosses from an Old Manse* he reviewed in 1842 and 1847.

In these essays, Poe ranked the tale as the supreme form for fiction, a place commonly given to the novel. For him, the compactness of the tale made possible both high excitement in the reader and maximum artistic control by the writer. Defined as a "short prose narrative, requiring from a half-hour to one or two hours in its perusal," the tale could be read in a single session, without the distraction of worldly pressures to break its hold on the reader's imagination. As one reads a novel over several sittings, by contrast, "external or extrinsic influences" intervene, Poe said, and the work cannot achieve "the immense force derivable from *totality*." In the tale, as not in the novel, the reader could be placed under the spell of an unbroken enchantment. And the brevity of the tale allowed the writer to strive for what Poe regarded as a "point of the greatest importance," the "unity of effect or impression."[10]

In defining this quality unique to the tale and the lyric poem, Poe drew on two terms given currency by the German scholar-poet August Wilhelm von Schlegel: "Einheit des Interesse" (unity of interest) and "Gesammt Eindruck" (totality of impression). The large meaning of these terms to Poe becomes clear in a restatement of them by the British aesthetician Archibald Alison. "In all the Fine Arts," Alison wrote, "that Composition is most excellent, in which the different parts most fully unite in the production of one unmingled Emotion, and that Taste the most perfect, where the perception of this relation of objects, in point of expression, is most delicate and precise."[11] In the well written tale, imagery, sentence rhythm, characterization, indeed every facet serves a single "preconceived effect" of horror, passion, sarcasm, or whatever. (Like most writers of the Romantic period, Poe stressed originality, which he understood as the writer's choosing for his "effect" some dimly experienced but so far unarticulated state of feeling, "bringing out the half-formed, the reluctant, or the unexpressed fancies of mankind.")[12] Poe left the tale writer no room for being offhand or sloppy: "In the whole composition there should be no word written, of which the tendency, direct or indirect, is not to the one pre-established design."[13]

With its emphasis on "the one pre-established design," Poe's theory of the art of the tale is profoundly teleological. Rhythm and punctuation must reinforce the effect of the words, the words the effect of the sentence, the sentence the effect of the narrative moment, and all must enhance the total effect. Only tales that adapt each element to the other, subordinating them all to a single effect can produce, Poe observed, the "fullest satisfaction." The discriminating reader will judge the tale intrinsically and relationally, considering, for instance, whether the kind of pause afforded by a semicolon in a particular place adumbrates and heightens the action being narrated, and whether both are in keeping with the overall effect intended. "The true critic will but demand that the design intended be accomplished, to the fullest extent, by the means most advantageously applicable."[14]

Yet Poe recognized that the means could never be adapted to the effect all pervasively. To achieve a tale in which every word, sentence rhythm, and structural device expresses a single end, in which everything depends on everything else – a tale entirely present at every moment in every word – lies beyond human ability, requiring a structural mega-memory and a transcendent ingenuity. In his treatise on the cosmos, *Eureka*, Poe wrote that only Divine Art could achieve this "absolute *reciprocity of adaptation*":

> [P]*erfection* of plot is really, or practically, unattainable – but only because it is a finite intelligence that constructs. The plots of God are perfect. The Universe is a plot of God.[15]

For Poe the tale, like all other forms of art, can only evoke this divine beauty, but can never embody it by achieving an infinite perfection of infinite interrelationships. In the same way, only angels and other perfect creatures can truly perceive beauty, a view that Poe memorably formulated in a later sketch, "The Domain of

Arnheim," as "the death-refined appreciation of the beautiful" (1274).

As Poe's comments about unity suggest, he scorned the Romantic idea that the artist creates spontaneously, powered by inspiration. He spoke rather of "the *analytical love of beauty*" and once said that he wanted to write a poem about the quadrature of curves.[16] In a famous passage from "The Philosophy of Composition" he compared the writer to an actor, who relies on the machinery of his craft to contrive his effect:

> Most writers – poets in especial – prefer having it understood that they compose by a species of fine frenzy – an ecstatic intuition – and would positively shudder at letting the public take a peep behind the scenes . . . at the cautious selections and rejections – at the painful erasures and interpolations – in a word, at the wheels and pinions – the tackle for scene-shifting – the step-ladders and demon-traps – the cock's feathers, the red paint and the black patches, which, in ninety-nine cases out of the hundred, constitute the properties of the literary *histrio*.[17]

Poe viewed the writer as a technician or craftsman, who, while his characters rage or swoon, coolly stands by calculating how to convey their emotions to the reader.

Much as he emphasized technique and the dynamic inner relationships of literary works, "the *analytical love of beauty*," Poe also deemphasized moral, religious, political, and social issues. These he consigned to sermons, journalism, philosophy, history, and similar works, ruling them out of imaginative writing. Characters in a tale may of course espouse socialism or devaluate Leonardo da Vinci's *Last Supper*, but the test of such ideas and opinions, for Poe, has nothing to do with their truth. They should be judged by their "adaptation" to the character depicted and to the overall effect. The fundamental error of using fiction or poetry as a vehicle for instruction rather than pleasure he called "The heresy of *The Didactic*."[18] Unlike the tales of many of his contemporaries, Poe's never preach; the critic Allen Tate classified him as a literary decadent for achieving a high intensity that lacks a moral dimension.

Poe particularly opposed placing fiction in the service of national pride. He wrote at a time when many American readers and writers were calling on the country to establish a literary independence

11

matching its political independence from England. Many insisted on the use of distinctively American characters, settings, and subjects. In Emerson's famous complaint, "We have listened too long to the courtly muses of Europe."[19] Poe opposed this literary nationalism. "That an American should confine himself to American themes, or even prefer them," he wrote, "is rather a political than a literary idea – and at best a questionable point." On the contrary, he argued, distance lends enchantment, and a "foreign theme is, in a strictly literary sense, to be preferred." While his contemporaries demanded American works drawn from the realities of American life, Poe championed the older, eighteenth-century ideal of the republic of letters, of a community of writers that cuts across boundaries of nation and of time. "After all," he wrote, and often repeated, "the world at large is the only legitimate stage for the autorial [*sic*] *histrio*."[20]

In choosing subjects and themes for his tales, Poe therefore rarely wrote about the contemporary scene. His fiction offers no glimpse of the whirlwind social changes wrought in nineteenth-century America by the development of steamboats and railroads, inventions like the daguerreotype and telegraph, and hot debates over women's rights, the ending of capital punishment, and the abolition of slavery. His very few tales that comment on contemporary life, such as "Mellonta Tauta" and "Some Words with a Mummy," disdainfully satirize it. Raised in the slaveholding South, he despised the abolitionists; disinherited by his foster father and never able to earn a decent living, he scorned the energies of democratic capitalism. He attacked the business culture and its pursuit of the dollar for corrupting taste, derided churchgoing as "the worship of two idols ... by the names of Wealth and Fashion," and burlesqued the belief in progress as illusory (1303). Egalitarian ideals and practices he saw as contrary to the hierarchical nature of the moral and physical universe. He denounced voting as meddling with public affairs and called democracy "a very admirable form of government – for dogs" (1300).

Poe not only theorized about fiction; he also applied his ideas in his tales. Although the pressures of the journalistic marketplace often compelled him to write much and fast, his best tales deserve study for their formal invention and technical nicety alone. His experiments in writing narratives within narratives ("Arthur Gordon Pym") or in combining fictional narrative with the journal ("Hans Phaal"), the essay ("The Imp of the Perverse"), and the newspaper article ("The Mystery of Marie Rogêt") have the self-referential feel of much postmodern fiction. He framed his narratives, too, between arresting openings and strong endings that first coax readers into the tale, then leave them with a memorable impression of it.

Often Poe began a tale with several repetitions of its key word. "Hop-Frog," for instance, concerns a dwarf who in revenge for being mocked by the king incinerates him and his advisers. In a tale about its protagonist's sensitivity to slights and derision, therefore, the first paragraph repeats the word *joke* or its variants no fewer than eight times.

> I never knew any one so keenly alive to a joke as the king was. He seemed to live only for joking. To tell a good story of the joke kind, and to tell it well, was the surest road to his favor. Thus it happened that his seven ministers were all noted for their accomplishments as jokers. They all took after the king, too, in being large, corpulent, oily men, as well as inimitable jokers. Whether people grow fat by joking, or whether there is something in fat itself which predisposes to a joke, I have never been quite able to determine; but certain it is that a lean joker is a *rara avis in terris.* (1345)

In concluding his tales Poe frequently used what might be called the copulative ending. From the classical rhetorical figure of polysyndeton, a repetition of conjunctions, he devised a trick of composing the final sentence or two as a series of "and" clauses, arranged to emphasize each element, as at the end of "The Masque of the Red Death":

> And now was acknowledged the presence of the Red Death . . . And one by one dropped the revellers in the blood-bedewed halls of their revel, and died each in the despairing posture of his fall. And the life of the ebony clock went out with that of the last of the gay. And the flames of the tripods expired. And Darkness and Decay and the Red Death held illimitable dominion over all. (677)

The *ands* are contrived to call attention to each detail individually – the dropping of the revellers, their postures, the stopped clocks, the extinguished flames, the darkness, the decay, and the dominion

13

of death, the reiterated d's further emphasizing each element by their thump.

Several of Poe's tales are told by characters involved in the action, whose manner of speaking reveals what they are like, and he fashioned syntax and rhythm to dramatize the storyteller's personality, especially in suggesting psychopathology. He rendered the mental disorder of the narrator of "The Tell-Tale Heart," for instance, by overemphasis, inversion, and lurching sentence rhythms: "TRUE! – nervous – very, very dreadfully nervous I had been and am" (792). Poe often supported the mood and action of his tales by such rhythmic and sound effects, drawing on the devices of lyric poetry. In his early tale "Berenice," a flurry of t's points up a moment of quiet hesitance: "a light tap at the library door – and, pale as the tenant of a tomb, a menial entered upon tiptoe" (218). In vivifying the savagery that erupts in some tales, an influential precursor to modern films of violence, he used chillingly flat declarative sentences: "I withdrew my arm from her grasp and buried the axe in her brain" (856); "I dismembered the corpse. I cut off the head and the arms and the legs" (796).

Perhaps Poe's most inventive and sustained use of such effects appears in "The Pit and the Pendulum." The narrator recounts his feelings while under sentence of death in a blackened dungeon, where a descending, razor-sharp pendulum threatens to slice him apart. His inability to see in the darkness occasions a technical tour de force: Poe describes the action not in terms of what is seen but in terms of smell, touch, and especially sound. The narrator experiences the descending blade largely by how it "*hissed* as it swung through the air" (690). Poe keeps the menacing pendulum aurally present for the reader by deploying sibilant words and phrases like "cessation," "crescent," and "coarse serge." Beginning with the opening line ("I was sick – sick unto death") scarcely a sentence fails to contain some buzzing or hissing sound, illustrating his doctrine of unity of effect: "I proceeded for many paces; but still all was blackness and vacancy" (685); "I succeeded in dislodging a small fragment, and let it fall into the abyss" (687); "The odor of the sharp steel forced itself into my nostrils" (691); "the boldest . . . smelt at the surcingle" (694); "I saw them fashion the syllables of my name; and I shuddered because no sound

14

succeeded" (681); "With a steady movement – cautious, sidelong, shrinking, and slow – I slid from the embrace of the bandage and beyond the sweep of the scimitar" (695).

Poe in His Tales

Critics have differed sharply in their evaluation of Poe. Among the detractors, Henry James considered an enthusiasm for Poe's work "the mark of a decidedly primitive stage of reflection"; T. S. Eliot granted Poe a powerful intellect, but added that it seemed "the intellect of a highly gifted young person before puberty"; F. O. Matthiessen, in his monumental study of nineteenth-century American Literature, *American Renaissance,* ignored Poe altogether.[21] On the other hand, Baudelaire, Dostoyevsky, Freud, Thomas Mann, and D. H. Lawrence all saw in Poe's tales a profound delineation of the disintegrated modern psyche. (In general, Poe has won fewer critical admirers in America than in other countries, especially France.) Critics have also variously identified Poe's deepest preoccupations, locating the core of his tales in different places: in their study of incest, doubling, and other aspects of human psychology; their satire of Romantic and Gothic convention; their formalist manner and self-reflexive interest in the process of reading and writing; their fascination with illusion and deception; and not least in their creation of horror and disgust.

Poe's tales do intricately encompass all these cores of significance, but no purely textual study of the tales – to return where we began – can account for the widespread sense of the writer and his writing as a single thing. Many of the recurrent motifs, dramatic conflicts, and themes of Poe's tales arose from intimate circumstances of his life.

Poe wrote some of his tales in immediate response to jolting personal events. "The Masque of the Red Death," for example, a story drenched in blood, appeared soon after his young wife's first hemorrhages. "The Cask of Amontillado," a reverberant tale of revenge, followed the many attacks on him during the New York newspaper wars. Readers familar with important names, dates, and places in Poe's early life will find them frequently embedded in the tales. He gave the two William Wilsons his own birthday,

15

January 19, and the year of his birth, 1809. The theatrical ambience of his first years figures not only generally through many allusions to singing, dancing, and acting, but most particularly as well. For "The Fall of the House of Usher" he borrowed the names of Noble Luke Usher and Harriet L'Estrange Usher, a husband-and-wife team with whom David and Eliza Poe had frequently acted. Perhaps most remarkably, in the unfinished tale about a lighthouse keeper which he probably wrote before his last trip to Virginia, Poe dated the final action of the tale on January 3, 1796, the same date and the same year on which his English-born mother had first arrived in America. The fact of Eliza Poe's death is especially prominent in the tales. The fifteen-year-old baron of "Metzengerstein" has been orphaned early in life: "His father, the Minister G——, died young. His mother, the Lady Mary, followed him quickly." As Poe may have done, the baron "stood, without a living relative, by the coffin of his dead mother. He laid his hand upon her placid forehead" (20). Poe's tales contain many such coffin-viewing scenes, and numerous boxes, crates, and coffin-like enclosures.*

Poe's tales replay the more shocking events of his life not only through isolated details and motifs but also in their larger actions and themes. Given the number and variety of his tales, and his insistence that artistic value resides in the mutual adaptation of parts, it would be crude to reduce all his fiction to a few plot patterns or kernels of meaning. Nevertheless, whether writing in the Gothic or ratiocinative modes, whether relating hair-raising adventures or slapstick domestic events, Poe concerned himself above all with death. In nearly every one of his tales, characters

---

*Poe similarly rehearsed his new existence under the Allan family. In "The Murders in the Rue Morgue" he quoted the testimony of a laundress named "Pauline Dubourg," fetching from memory the "Misses Dubourg" under whom he had been educated while the Allans lived in England. In a sketch entitled "Why the Little Frenchman Wears His Hand in a Sling," he placed his narrator at "39 Southampton Row, Russell Square," the Allans' actual London address. And his adolescent battles with John Allan often seem recapitulated in such tales of rivalry between an older and a younger man as "Three Sundays in a Week," in which the ungiving Uncle Rumgudgeon, who has a "profound contempt" for literature, threatens to disinherit the nephew he has raised after the death of the nephew's parents.

confront death, and sometimes annihilation. Not all the kinds of death or their implications can be discussed here, but generally speaking, Poe's preoccupation gave rise to two types of dramatic action, narratives that treat either the devastating loss of a beloved woman, or the fate of the self in the afterlife. Each of these perspectives on death – mourning and survival – can be illustrated through the summary of a paradigmatic tale.

The unnamed storyteller of ''The Oblong Box'' (1844) recounts his voyage aboard a packet-ship from Charleston, South Carolina, to New York City. Among the passengers he finds his acquaintance Cornelius Wyatt, a young artist, newly married. To his surprise, he finds Wyatt morose and his bride vulgar. When he observes that she sleeps in a separate stateroom, he concludes that the couple are contemplating divorce. Each night he hears subdued noises coming from Wyatt's own room, with murmuring or sobbing. He had noticed that, just before sailing, an oblong box had been delivered to Wyatt, ''about six feet in length by two and a half in breadth'' (925). He thinks it must contain a copy of Leonardo's *Last Supper,* and that the subdued noise from the stateroom must represent the artist prying it open with a chisel and muffled mallet. Although he cannot explain the sobbing noises, he believes that Wyatt uncovers the box nightly ''in order to feast his eyes on the pictorial treasure within'' (929).

After a week at sea the packet encounters a hurricane that forces the passengers to abandon ship in lifeboats. Wyatt refuses to accompany them unless he can take the oblong box with him. Despite the furious storm he rushes down into his cabin, by preternatural strength hauls the oblong box up the companionway, and lashes himself to it with a rope. He and the box are both swallowed up in the sea.

A month later, having escaped the shipwreck, the storyteller learns the truth of his friend's mysterious self-destruction. Before the packet embarked, the artist's wife had suddenly died. The captain realized that the superstitious passengers would refuse to sail with a dead body aboard; he arranged for the corpse to be partly embalmed and conveyed as merchandise. Wyatt's servant acted as his wife, sleeping in a separate stateroom. Pried open, the box revealed to the artist as he watched all night not his copy of

17

Leonardo, but a different sort of "pictorial treasure," the remains of his dead wife. Rather than abandon her corpse, he accompanied it to the bottom of the sea.

Such is Poe's tale of devastating bereavement, the "unutterable wo," as he put it in "Ligeia," following the loss of "the one only and supremely beloved" (326). The death of a beloved woman forms the main action of some of Poe's best known tales, including "Berenice," "Morella," "Ligeia," "Eleonora," "The Fall of the House of Usher," and "The Oval Portrait," and figures prominently also in "The Assignation," "The Mystery of Marie Rogêt," "The Murders in the Rue Morgue," and "The Black Cat," among others.

Like Cornelius Wyatt, the characters in many of these tales remain mournfully tied to the past. Poe is particularly effective in dramatizing their failure to work through feelings of attachment, or to put them at bay by displacement, repression, projection, and similar psychological mechanisms. The narrator of "Morella," for instance, feels compelled, at the christening of his ten-year-old daughter, to blurt out the name of his dead wife, although many other names occur to him: "What prompted me, then, to disturb the memory of the buried dead? What demon urged me to breathe that sound?" (235) All unknowingly, the husband in "Berenice" sleepwalks to the grave of his wife and pulls out her teeth for mementoes; when he awakens the next morning he finds beside his bed an opened book which he has underscored, also unknowingly, at the sentence: "My companions told me I might find some little alleviation of my misery, in visiting the grave of my beloved" (218). No more than the pestilence can be kept from Prince Prospero's castle in "The Masque of the Red Death" can the deep meaning of the past be kept from consciousness. Like the treasure unearthed in "The Gold-Bug" or the murdered old man exhumed from under the floorboards in "The Tell-Tale Heart," painful memories of Poe's characters fail to stay buried, but reappear despite conscious control.

Aside from the simple fact that it is not so easy to put behind one objects that have inspired love or horror, Poe's tales offer varying explanations for this strangling allegiance to those who have been loved and lost. Many of his protagonists suffer from guilt and think of remarriage as disloyalty to the dead. The narrator

18

Introduction

of "Eleonora" vows "that I would never bind myself in marriage to any daughter of Earth – that I would in no manner prove recreant to her dear memory" (642). Other characters cannot overcome their loss because they feel totally dependent on the beloved. Ligeia's husband looks to his wife for guidance with "child-like confidence," as if she were a parent. Like the artist of "The Oblong Box," some of the bereaved prefer to join the dead. Many characters in Poe's tales reveal urges for self-destruction, such as Arthur Gordon Pym, who, when he gazes into an abyss, experiences *"a longing to fall;* a desire, a yearning, a passion utterly uncontrollable."[22]

The sources of Poe's preoccupation with the death of a beautiful woman have already been sketched here. Much as the artist Wyatt kept his wife's corpse in his stateroom, Poe retained the presence of his mother, Eliza Poe, dead at the age of twenty-four – an enduring shock reinforced by the death of his foster mother Fanny Allan at the age of forty-four, and of his wife Virginia at the age of twenty-five. As his childlike closeness with Sissy and "Mother"-Muddy and his frantic difficulties in remarrying suggest, he too felt greatly dependent and suffered the guilt of disloyalty. (An acquaintance remarked, coldly but accurately, that he was "incapable of taking care of himself.")[23] America during Poe's time reinforced his iron bond to the dead in creating a "cult of memory."[24] With the rapid pace of nineteenth-century life, the cash mentality of the business culture, the removal of cemeteries from the centers of growing cities to the outskirts, many Americans complained that the dead were being neglected and forgotten. In resisting these tides, they photographed relatives and friends in death or kept locks of their hair. From American publishers, newspapers, and magazines came scores of consolatory books on mourning, countless poems on death, the dead, and dying. The literary quality of such works rarely rose above a stilted tearfulness. Yet the bottomless appetite for hearing about death also provided a public subject that focused the profound imaginations of Walt Whitman and Emily Dickinson.

A desire to preserve the dead perhaps accounts for a particular feature of "The Oblong Box" that recurs often in Poe's tales, although it seems remote from death and mourning. The artist's

19

drowning is one of many instances of engulfment. "MS. Found in a Bottle" ends with the narrator plunging into a whirlpool, about to be "swallowed up at once and for ever" (143); the narrator of "A Descent into the Maelström" is drawn into a vast oceanic funnel, "in the very jaws of the gulf" (588). As the words "swallowed" and "jaws" suggest, these images of engulfment are part of a still larger network of images having to do with biting, devouring, and similar oral mutilation. The young baron of "Metzengerstein" has "the fangs of a petty Caligula" (21) and rides to his death with "lacerated lips, which were bitten through and through" (29); the vengeful dwarf of the late tale "Hop-Frog" maniacally grinds his "large, powerful, and very repulsive teeth" (1349). Such examples can be multiplied without end, for hardly a tale of Poe's lacks chomping teeth, ravaging hunger, consuming fire, engulfing vortexes.

Current psychoanalytic thinking about childhood bereavement explains the fantasy of being swallowed up as representing a desire, mixed with dread, to merge with the dead; the wish to devour represents a primitive attempt at preserving loved ones, incorporating them so as not to lose them. The devil in Poe's comic tale "Bon-Bon" eats with relish the souls of Plato, Aristophanes, and others – toasted, pickled, or fricaseed – and Pym and his shipmates cannibalize one of their companions. To this network of images also belong Poe's omnipresent descriptions of large eyes, which, like teeth, take in others. When the axe murderer of "The Black Cat" is bitten by his cat's teeth, he cuts out its eye, as if teeth and eyes were equal. The narrator of "Morella" makes the equation between seeing and swallowing up explicit: "I met the glance of her meaning eyes, and then my soul sickened and became giddy with the giddiness of one who gazes downward into some dreary and unfathomable abyss" (232–3). Poe's universe of those desperate to preserve lost loves is thus peopled with characters who chew and gnaw and eye hungrily.

"The Oblong Box" itself, finally, declares the source of the artistic impulse that generated many of Poe's tales. Its protagonist is after all an artist, and the corpse over which he sobs is mistaken for a copy of Leonardo's *Last Supper,* implying a similarity between mourning and art. Poe gave this notion a vampirish turn in "The

Oval Portrait," a tale-within-a-tale concerning a painter who induces his wife to pose for him day after day, until she grows dispirited, weak, and finally dies: "the tints which he spread upon the canvass [sic] were drawn from the cheeks of her who sat beside him" (665). In writing his tales Poe, too, nourished himself on a young woman's death, in the sense that art was for him a form of mourning, a revisitation of his past and of what he had lost, as if trying to make them right. Since nothing could, he returned to the subject of "the one only and supremely beloved" again and again.

The second type of dramatic action common in Poe's tales concerns the survival of the self after death. It can be illustrated through one of his "*post-mortem* reveries," "The Colloquy of Monos and Una" (1841). Two spirits, once lovers on earth, are reunited a century after their passing. In a long monologue, Monos describes for Una his journey from life to death into the life beyond death. He recalls that with the cessation of his heart and breathing, his senses became unusually active although eccentric, assuming each other's functions. Taste and smell became confounded; he perceived images as sounds. Indeed all his perceptions became purely sensual, unmediated by the deceased understanding, a sensing without knowing. With the onset of bodily decay arose a sort of sixth sense, analogous to the human sense of time but independent of events, "a mental pendulous pulsation. . . . [a] keen, perfect, self-existing sentiment of *duration*" (615). Monos recalls how, as weeks and months passed in the grave, his new consciousness somehow became transferred to his environment: "The narrow space immediately surrounding what had been the body, was now growing to be the body itself" (616). Ultimately his sense of being someone evolved into a sense of being some-place and some-time or, rather, of being a place-conscious place and time-conscious time.

To thus distill Poe's somberly lyrical "colloquy" into a few statements saps the force of his attempt to suggest how the self, in attaining a new mode of consciousness, can endure after dying. But for the sake of identifying a widespread pattern in his tales, what matters here is the attempt itself. As a keen French critic, Charles de Moüy, remarked in 1863, Poe "questions the tomb; he tries to penetrate the stone under which the dead lie and to discover the fate of our tormented souls."[25] Hardly a tale by Poe, in whatever form or mood, fails to dramatize some means by which one can die and still live. "Metzengerstein" turns on the transmigration of the soul into a new human or animal shape, as the murdered old Count is weirdly reborn into a gigantic horse depicted on a tapestry, which springs to life, eyes aglow. Ernest Valdemar, of "The Facts in the Case of M. Valdemar," suffers from a fatal consumption; when about to die he is placed by a mesmerist in a state of suspended animation. Showing no vital signs, he declares "*I am dead.*" William Wilson plunges his sword through his double, also named William Wilson, but finds that "William Wilson" survives, that his double is himself, or vice versa. In the comic tale "The Psyche Zenobia," the hand of a huge steeple clock descends on the female protagonist's neck, popping her eyes out and then severing her head; but, assuming lives of their own, the detached eyeballs wink, the truncated head takes snuff.

Whether by metempsychosis, mesmerism, twinship, or sheer unkillableness, the characters of Poe's tales repeatedly overcome death. As he insists in "The Pit and the Pendulum," "even in the grave all *is not* lost" (682). This denial of death is ancient and commonplace in Western culture, where people paint the dead to look as in life and continue to select comfortable coffins for them. The situation in Poe is more complex and surprising, however. In some tales, such as "The Oblong Box," people do in fact die, and in many others they are reborn only to die again. The newly wed hero of the farcical "Loss of Breath" manages to remain alive after losing his ability to breathe, but then fractures his skull and breaks his thighs; comes alive again but is laid out for burial; survives that but is hanged; lives once more but is eviscerated, and lives yet again, "kicking and plunging with all my might" – repeatedly dying and being revived (67). Poe even extended this vision of serial births and deaths to all of nature. His philosophical treatise *Eureka* (1848) depicts the cosmos as being composed of an infinitude of universes collapsing into an original nothingness, only to be reborn again and then to collapse again, ad infinitum: "a novel Universe swelling into existence, and then subsiding into nothingness, at every throb of the Heart Divine."[26]

Poe's tales, then, sometimes treat death as final, sometimes as an entry to eternal life, and sometimes as part of a succession of deaths. The differing outcomes record how anxiously he wrestled with broader nineteenth-century questionings about the ultimate fate of the self in the wake of the collapse of traditional Christianity, trying, as many others did also, to find plausible alternatives for long-held religious beliefs.

They also record – to draw again on psychoanalytic ideas – something more personal: In failing to come to terms with the early death of his mother, he faroff maintained the belief that she might return to him, or that he might join her in some afterworld. Paradoxically, most of Poe's tales present a simultaneous belief and disbelief in the return of the dead. Such splitting, to use the psychoanalytic term, typifies what has been called "established mourning."[27] Whereas adults learn through a long and painful process of mourning to withdraw the feelings they have invested in the loved one, children, according to current psychoanalytic thought, are unable to mourn. What prevents them is an inability to grasp the concept of death. They have come to depend on the dead parent for physical and emotional support and cannot endure the pain of renunciation. They therefore go on behaving as though the loved one were alive and might return, a state which in "established mourners" endures at some level throughout life. Thus in Poe's world things are most often, as the narrator of "Loss of Breath" puts it, "alive, with the qualifications of the dead – dead, with the propensities of the living" (63).

This split attitude reveals itself through many facets of the tales. Characters and places are not only both dead and not dead, but also at the same time inanimate and animate, natural and artificial, material and immaterial, mechanical and organic. To choose "MS. Found in a Bottle," from among many examples, the captain of the strange ship seems both young and old: "His forehead, although little wrinkled, seems to bear upon it the stamp of a myriad of years." His speech seems both far and near: "although . . . close at my elbow, yet his voice seemed to reach my ears from the distance of a mile" (144). Such paradoxes mark Poe's world on the largest scale too: When the universe of *Eureka* disappears again into nothingness, it becomes, he says, "Matter without Matter" or "Material Nihility." Readers who enjoy Poe are also likely to feel attuned to the paintings of the Belgian surrealist René Magritte (1898–1967), who similarly lost his mother (by drowning) when young. No other paintings come so close as Magritte's to rendering visible the yes-and-no, dead-and-alive atmosphere of Poe's fiction. On Magritte's canvases women are at once living beings and statues or coffins; the sky is both natural and painted; panes of glass appear to be simultaneously transparent windows and reflecting mirrors. His painting of a tobacco pipe has the caption "This is not a pipe."

Pointing out these oxymoronic signs of "established mourning" does not reduce Poe's tales to pathology but accounts for one element of their appeal. For much of their power lies in their ability to reawaken magical beliefs we all had as children and have never wholly abandoned, uncanny feelings that dumb objects can come to life, that we may be eaten and devoured, that the dead can return.

That appeal continues, as the following critical essays attest. Their authors address features of Poe's major tales that are conspicuously intriguing and enigmatic. Christopher Benfey aligns Poe with modern philosophers who have pondered the problem of whether we can understand what other people feel. He shows how "The Tell-Tale Heart" and "The Black Cat" dramatize the opposite but equal dangers of complete isolation and unqualified love. Louise J. Kaplan analyzes the "perverse strategy" operating in "The Fall of the House of Usher" – Poe's use of symbolic forms to ventilate forbidden feelings whose direct expression would threaten the moral order. David Van Leer finds in the ingenious detective work of Poe's Dupin tales a more general interest in the question of what constitutes truth, and in the subtle means by which truth may be suppressed. Although Poe's fictional world usually seems to mirror no particular place or time, David S. Reynolds demonstrates that such tales as "The Cask of Amontillado" draw on literary forms of mid-nineteenth-century American popular culture, and reflect social issues of the period. In the final essay, J. Gerald Kennedy returns to some of the matter of this Introduction, but gives it a different interpretation. He stresses how Poe's fictional treatment of the deaths of beloved women, especially in "Ligeia," betrays an underlying revulsion and rage that necessarily accompany adoration.

NOTES

1 The following account of Poe's life is based on my biography, *Edgar A. Poe: Mournful and Never-ending Remembrance* (New York: Harper-Collins, 1991).
2 Ibid., p. 63.
3 Ibid., p. 415.
4 *The Letters of Edgar Allan Poe*, ed. John Ward Ostrom, rev. ed. (New York: Gordian Press, 1966), vol. 2, p. 329.
5 *Collected Works of Edgar Allan Poe*, ed. Thomas Ollive Mabbott (Cambridge: Harvard University Press, 1978), p. 1103. All further quotations from Poe's tales are from this edition. Page numbers are indicated within parentheses in the text.
6 *Edgar Allan Poe: Essays and Reviews*, ed. G. R. Thompson (New York: The Library of America, 1984), p. 871.
7 Ibid., p. 872.
8 Ibid., p. 869.
9 Ibid., p. 226.
10 Ibid., pp. 571–2.
11 Quoted in Robert D. Jacobs, *Poe: Journalist & Critic* (Baton Rouge: Louisiana State University Press, 1969), pp. 321–2.
12 *Essays and Reviews*, p. 581.
13 Ibid., p. 586.
14 Ibid., p. 573.
15 *Edgar Allan Poe: Poetry and Tales*, ed. Patrick F. Quinn (New York: The Library of America, 1984), pp. 1354, 1342.
16 *Collected Writings of Edgar Allan Poe*, ed. B. R. Pollin (New York: Gordian Press, 1985), vol. 2, p. 131.
17 *Essays and Reviews*, p. 14.
18 Ibid., p. 75.
19 "The American Scholar," in *The Works of Ralph Waldo Emerson* (Boston and New York: [Ticknor & Fields], 1909), vol. 1, p. 113.
20 *The Broadway Journal*, 2 (October 4, 1845), 199.
21 *The Recognition of Edgar Allan Poe: Selected Criticism Since 1829*, ed. Eric W. Carlson (Ann Arbor: University of Michigan Press, 1966), pp. 66, 212.
22 *Poetry and Tales*, p. 1170.
23 *Edgar A. Poe*, p. 359.
24 See, for instance, Ann Douglas, *The Feminization of American Culture* (rpt. New York: Doubleday, 1988), ch. 6, "The Domestication of Death."

145,799

25 "Contemporary Studies—Edgar Poe," in *Affidavits of Genius: Edgar Allan Poe and the French Critics, 1847–1924,* ed. Jean Alexander (Port Washington, N.Y.: Kennikat Press, 1971), p. 164.

26 *Poetry and Tales,* p. 1356.

27 On childhood bereavement see, for instance, the essays in *The Problem of Loss and Mourning: Psychoanalytic Perspectives,* ed. David R. Dietrich and Peter C. Shabad (Madison, Conn.: International Universities Press, 1989).

2

Poe and the Unreadable: "The Black Cat" and "The Tell-Tale Heart"

CHRISTOPHER BENFEY

> Two fears should follow us through life. There is the fear that we shan't prove worthy in the eyes of someone who knows us at least as well as we know ourselves. That is the fear of God. And there is the fear of Man – the fear that men won't understand us and we shall be cut off from them.
>
> –Robert Frost[1]

POE aimed to puzzle his readers. Tale after tale begins or ends with an invitation to decode or decipher a peculiar sequence of events. Some of Poe's most memorable characters are themselves solvers of riddles – amateur scientists, private detectives, armchair philosophers who glorify in what Poe calls "that moral activity which *disentangles.*"[2] The modern-day Oedipus, according to Poe, "is fond of enigmas, of conundrums, of hieroglyphics; exhibiting in his solutions of each a degree of *acumen* which appears to the ordinary apprehension praeternatural" (528).

Poe's critics have tended to divide into two camps: on the one hand, those who claim to have keys to the puzzles, and on the other, those who find the puzzles impossible or unworthy of solution. In the first group one finds a wealth of extraordinary psychoanalytic readings of Poe – surely no other writer other than Freud himself has so engaged the psychoanalytic literary community, from Marie Bonaparte's pioneering reading of Poe to Lacan's famous interpretation of "The Purloined Letter" and the further commentary it inspired. In the first group one also finds psychologically astute – though not explicitly psychoanalytic – readers like the poet Richard Wilbur, who finds in Poe's tales representations of the ordinary phases of falling asleep.[3]

In the second group – the resistant readers – belong such dismissive critics as Harold Bloom, who claims to find Poe's prose literally unreadable. "Translation even into his own language," Bloom acidly remarks, "always benefits Poe."[4] To this group also belong such historically minded critics as David Reynolds, for whom Poe's puzzles are interesting primarily as literary conventions, the sort of lure for the masses that Poe, writing at mid-nineteenth century for a magazine-reading public, had no choice but to employ.[5]

I do not propose to steer a middle course between these two camps, even if it were easy to say what such a course might be. My aim instead is to show how one kind of puzzle — perhaps not the most obvious or "crackable" kind — is at the heart of some of Poe's best known tales. This sort of puzzle concerns the ways in which people are themselves enigmas to one another: people (that is characters) both within the stories and on either side, so to speak (the author and the reader). Poe was an early student of the ways in which human beings have access, or are denied access, to the minds of other people. Twentieth-century philosophers such as Ludwig Wittgenstein and J. L. Austin have devoted a good deal of attention to what has come to be called "the problem of other minds," trying to answer the arguments of skeptics who claim, for example, that we cannot know for certain that another person is in pain. Poe's tales, it seems to me, address such questions from oblique and unexpected angles. If figures from as divergent cultural and historical milieux as Poe and Freud can be invited into useful dialogue, the same could be said for Poe and Wittgenstein. (The latter, by the way, came of age in precisely the same turn-of-the-century Viennese culture as did Freud.)

Poe was fascinated by mind readers and unreadable faces, the twin fantasies of utter exposure and complete secrecy. His private eye Auguste Dupin is the preeminent example of the former. In a scene from "The Murders in the Rue Morgue," Dupin astonishes the narrator by reading his mind, having boasted that "most men, in respect to himself, wore windows in their bosoms" (533). Dupin pulls off this feat by being extraordinarily attentive to psychological association, a process Poe relates to the solving of puzzling crimes. In "The Purloined Letter," Dupin retrieves the hidden letter by reproducing the mental calculations of the deceitful minister D. The devil, in the less familiar story "Bon-Bon," has kindred powers — he can even read the mind of a pet cat (a subject to which we will return).

Poe was equally interested, however, in the opposite phenomenon of the unknowable mind, the mind that remains, despite all attempts at access, ultimately mysterious. One of his best known tales, "The Man of the Crowd" – it drew commentary from Baudelaire as well as from the great modern critic Walter Benjamin – begins and ends by comparing certain people to the sort of book that "does not permit itself to be read":

> Men die nightly in their beds, wringing the hands of ghostly confessors, and looking them piteously in the eyes – die with despair of heart and convulsion of throat, on account of the hideousness of mysteries which will not *suffer themselves* to be revealed. (506–7)

It is to this theme of the unreadable in human relations that my subtitle refers. It is not by accident that Poe should invite us to compare reading minds with reading books, or that his stories should involve both activities. He saw the most intimate relation between these two acts of reading, constantly drawing analogies between them. We will now turn to two such tales: "The Tell-Tale Heart" and "The Black Cat." We will also give some attention to a third text, a sort of hybrid of essay and tale entitled "The Imp of the Perverse."

These tales are not whodunits – we know right from the start who the murderer is. They are closer to the genre now called thrillers, where the crime itself and the psychology of the killer are more the focus than the question of who committed the crime. If there is a mystery in these tales, it is the mystery of motive: not who did it but why. Poe's fascination with the idea of a crime without a clear motive has proved to be one of his richest bequests to later writers, informing such works as Dostoevsky's *Crime and Punishment,* André Gide's *Lafcadio's Adventures* (*Les Caves du Vatican*), and Camus's *The Stranger,* all three of which test the idea that human freedom is most convincingly exhibited in an extreme and gratuitous act, specifically an act of murder with no obvious advantage to the murderer. Poe's interest in motiveless crime, however, had less to do with human freedom than with human knowledge. He was drawn to two ideas connected with it: one, the ways in which the murderer is a mystery to himself (a dominant idea in "The Black Cat"), and two, the related ways in which the

29

murder results from some barrier to the killer's knowledge of other people (a major theme in "The Tell-Tale Heart").

"The Tell-Tale Heart" begins *in medias res,* in the midst of things. We seem to be overhearing a conversation – one that began before our arrival on the scene – between a murderer and his interlocutor. The identity of the latter is never specified; it could be a prison warden, a doctor in a madhouse, a newspaper reporter, a judge. The very indefiniteness makes it easy for the reader to imagine that the killer is speaking directly to him or her.

> True! – nervous – very, very dreadfully nervous I had been and am; but why *will* you say that I am mad? The disease had sharpened my senses – not destroyed – not dulled them. Above all was the sense of hearing acute. I heard all things in the heaven and in the earth. I heard many things in hell. How, then, am I mad? Hearken! and observe how healthily – how calmly I can tell you the whole story. (792)

The first word is a concession – this speaker wants to communicate, to persuade. He thinks that by giving some ground ("granted I'm nervous"), he can win the battle ("but I'm not crazy").

Like other characters in Poe's tales (and to some degree, apparently, Poe himself), the narrator believes that certain diseases of the mind can actually sharpen mental acuity. In "Eleonora," for example, another half mad speaker tries to persuade us that he is sane: "Men have called me mad," he says, "but the question is not yet settled . . . whether all that is profound – does not spring from disease of thought – from *moods* of mind exalted at the expense of the general intellect" (638). And when the narrator of "The Murders in the Rue Morgue" tries to explain Dupin's extraordinary powers, he remarks: "What I have described in the Frenchman was merely the result of an excited, or perhaps of a diseased intelligence" (533). If the speaker in "The Tell-Tale Heart" is willing to admit that he's the victim of a disease, madness he will not concede. Like much else in the tale, the nature of the disease remains unspecified, unless it is the general nervousness that he mentions.

He does make perfectly clear what madness is. It is the inability to communicate. His proof of his sanity will therefore be his ability to "*tell*. . . the whole story" [my emphasis] – the verb is crucial – "healthily" and "calmly." Sanity is equated in this character's mind with telling tales. He invites us to gauge how healthily and calmly he can recount the story of the murder.

It is an extraordinary opening, with its mad dashes and nervous, halting delivery. Among his "Marginalia" Poe has preserved a miniature essay on the expressive powers of the dash. Always attentive to punctuation, he was especially fond of the dash, with its suggestion of mental leaps and quick associations. "It represents," he wrote, "a second thought – an emendation."[6] As our speaker begins his "calm" narrative, turning first to the question of motive, we are attuned to the contrasting rhythms of the dash, and we await its recurrence throughout the tale as a sort of trademark of this speaker's style.

> It is impossible to say how first the idea entered my brain; but, once conceived, it haunted me day and night. Object there was none. Passion there was none. I loved the old man. He had never wronged me. He had never given me insult. For his gold I had no desire. I think it was his eye! yes, it was this! One of his eyes resembled that of a vulture – a pale blue eye, with a film over it. Whenever it fell upon me, my blood ran cold; and so by degrees – very gradually – I made up my mind to take the life of the old man, and thus rid myself of the eye forever. (792)

Note how casually the speaker arrives at the eye as cause, as though he is casting about for the motive, and has just now thought of it – "I *think* it was his eye! yes, it was this!" [my emphasis] This is no ordinary eye, of course, but what exactly is so troubling about it? For one thing, it has "a film over it." There is something unseeing about it. When we look at someone "eye to eye" we feel in touch with the person, but this eye is blocked, filmed over. Richard Wilbur links this vulture eye with the vulture in Poe's early sonnet "To Science," in which Poe addresses the anti-imaginative spirit of science that changes "all things with thy peering eyes":

> Why preyest thou thus upon the poet's heart,
> Vulture, whose wings are dull realities?[7]

Wilbur wants to nudge us toward an allegorical reading of the tale, with the speaker-killer representing the imaginative faculty

31

of the mind and the old man representing the scientific, rational side.

But let us stay within the terms of the story a bit longer, before trying to arrive at its "larger meaning." We are never told the exact relationship between the old man and his killer. We never learn their names, their jobs, what town they live in, or anything much else about them. We simply know that they live together in the same house.

For all the concision with which our speaker tells his tale, eliminating almost every detail that would help us place him in time and space, he goes on at elaborate length about things that might seem peripheral to the main plot of the story. Nearly a quarter of the narrative, for example, is devoted to the seven nights in which the narrator watches the old man sleep. Why such sustained attention to such *undramatic* behavior?

According to the narrator, this patient observation is meant to provide further and conclusive proof of his sanity. All his preparations – the opened door, closed lantern, and so on – are so *deliberate* (a key word in both "The Black Cat" and "The Tell-Tale Heart") that no madman could have accomplished them.

> Now this is the point. You fancy me mad. Madmen know nothing. But you should have seen *me.* You should have seen how wisely I proceeded – with what caution – with what foresight – with what dissimulation I went to work! (792)

It is only in his account of the eighth and crucial night that Poe hints at the significance of this long rigmarole of door, lantern, and eye.

> Never, before that night, had I *felt* the extent of my own powers – of my sagacity. I could scarcely contain my feelings of triumph. To think that there I was, opening the door, little by little, and he not even to dream of my secret deeds or thoughts. I fairly chuckled at the idea; and perhaps he heard me; for he moved on the bed suddenly, as if startled. Now you may think that I drew back – but no. (793)

This is a crucial moment in the story. It shows how much the speaker's motivation has to do with secrecy, with keeping his thoughts hidden. (There is a remarkably similar moment of mute triumph in "The Black Cat": "The glee at my heart was too strong to be restrained. I burned to say if but one word, by way of triumph" [858].) He enters the old man's room night after night as a sort of ritual to establish this secrecy, this fact of human separateness.

And yet, for all his secrecy, our speaker claims to have access to the mind of the old man. His very privacy, his enclosedness, seem to allow him to see into the minds of other people.

> Presently I heard a slight groan, and I knew it was the groan of mortal terror. It was not a groan of pain or of grief – oh, no! – it was the low stifled sound that arises from the bottom of the soul when overcharged with awe. (794)

We may wonder how the speaker claims to know this. The answer, he tells us, is by analogy with his own experience and its expression:

> I knew the sound well. Many a night, just at midnight, when all the world slept, it has welled up from my own bosom, deepening with its dreadful echo, the terrors that distracted me. I say I knew it well. I knew what the old man felt, and pitied him, although I chuckled at heart. I knew that he had been lying awake ever since the first slight noise. (794)

This scene of mind reading continues a bit longer, as the killer claims to know the very words the victim is thinking:

> His fears had been ever since growing upon him. He had been trying to fancy them causeless, but could not. He had been saying to himself – "It is nothing but the wind in the chimney – it is only a mouse crossing the floor," or "it is merely a cricket which has made a single chirp." Yes, he has been trying to comfort himself with these suppositions: but he had found all in vain. (794)

It is only after this sustained scene of mind reading versus secrecy that the old man's eye opens, and the murder is accomplished. It is precisely the breach of secrecy, the penetrating-yet-veiled eye, that seems to motivate the murder.

Poe puts unmistakable emphasis on this claim to *knowledge*: "I say I *knew* it well. I *knew* what the old man felt. . . . I *knew* that he had been lying awake" [my emphasis]. It is precisely this claim to knowledge of another's mind, especially knowledge of another's feelings of pain, that has given rise to some of the most challenging philosophical reflections in our century. Wittgenstein, in a couple of classic passages in his *Philosophical Investigations*, defines the issues succinctly:

> 246. In what sense are my sensations *private?* — Well, only I can know whether I am really in pain: another person can only surmise it. — In one way this is wrong, and in another nonsense. If we are using the word "to know" as it is normally used (and how else are we to use it?), then other people very often know when I am in pain. — Yes, but all the same not with the certainty with which I know it myself! — It can't be said of me at all (except perhaps as a joke) that I *know* I am in pain. What is it supposed to mean — except perhaps that I *am* in pain?[8]

Wittgenstein, in his characteristically dialogical style, is challenging the skeptic's claim that we cannot "know" another's pain. Wittgenstein appeals to our ordinary use of language — "and how else are we to use it?" — as opposed to some special philosophical use, and argues that it's ridiculous to claim that we never can know that another is in pain. We know this — under ordinary circumstances (the stubbed toe, the woman in labor, the burst blister) — all the time. Wittgenstein, here and elsewhere, wants to cure us of our tendency to step outside our ordinary ways of living our lives, and our tendency to demand, for example, kinds of certainty that are inappropriate to our dealings with other people. (Poe seems to have something similar in mind when he insists that the events in "The Black Cat" are "ordinary.")

Poe's killers claim to have the very certainty challenged by Wittgenstein. They are always insisting on their special knowledge of others' minds, as though we had been challenging their knowledge: "I say I knew it well. I knew what the old man felt." The killer's claim, in "The Tell-Tale Heart," that he knows the man's feelings by analogy with his own — "I know that he feels x when he cries y because when I cry y I feel x" — is another of Wittgenstein's subjects:

> 302. If one has to imagine someone else's pain on the model of one's own, this is none too easy a thing to do: for I have to imagine pain which I *do not feel* on the model of the pain which I *do feel*. That is, what I have to do is not simply to make a transition in

imagination from one place of pain to another. As, from pain in the hand to pain in the arm. For I am not to imagine that I feel pain in some region of his body. (Which would also be possible.) Pain-behaviour can point to a painful place – but the subject of pain is the person who gives it expression.

Poe's killer makes oddly parallel claims: "I knew the sound well. Many a night, just at midnight, when all the world slept, it has welled up from my own bosom. . . . I say I knew it well. I knew what the old man felt." It does seem as though he is "imagining someone else's pain on the model of [his] own."

The skeptical view of ultimate human separateness ("We can never know for certain what another person is thinking or feeling") is intolerable to Poe's killers; their response is simply to deny it, even to the point of killing in order to prove their certainty. Rather than push the parallels between Poe and Wittgenstein further (perhaps we have already pushed them quite far enough), let us turn to another tale of murder and concealment, namely "The Black Cat." In comparing the two tales, especially their endings, we might find more to say about the two fears – of total exposure and total isolation – that Poe keeps giving voice to.

"The Black Cat" was first published later the same year, 1843, as "The Tell-Tale Heart." It resembles the earlier story in several obvious ways, as though Poe were digging deeper in a familiar vein. It too purports to be a killer's confession, and the murder victim is again a member of the killer's household. This killer is also eager to assure us of his sanity: "Yet, mad am I not – and very surely do I not dream." In both stories, furthermore, the police seem almost reluctant to pursue their investigations. The killers must insist on their guilt, even offer proof of it. In each case the discovery of the concealed body is the result of the killer's own obsessive need to reveal its hiding place.

The ways in which the two stories are told are quite distinct, however. One begins at the beginning ("From my infancy . . . I married early . . .") while the other begins in the midst of things. "The Tell-Tale Heart" purports to be a spoken narrative and much of its effect is achieved through the illusion of oral delivery. "The Black Cat," by contrast, presents itself from its opening sentence as a written narrative: "For the most wild, yet most homely narrative which I am about to pen, I neither expect nor solicit belief." What is more, the first of the narrator's series of crimes is explicitly linked to this writing instrument:

> I took from my waistcoat-pocket a *pen*-knife, opened it, grasped the poor beast by the throat, and deliberately cut one of its eyes from the socket! I blush, I burn, I shudder, while I *pen* the damnable atrocity. [my emphasis] (851)

The pen may be mightier than the sword, but in this passage Poe skillfully conflates the two. The weapon here is a pen-knife, which was used to sharpen a quill pen. Poe wants us to divine a connection between violence and the act of writing. (Similarly in "The Imp of the Perverse" the murder instrument is a poisoned candle used for *reading*.) Significantly, the murderer doesn't blush, burn, and shudder while committing the crime, but while writing about it later.

The link of pens and pen-knives points to a larger contrast in these tales. For the more we read and reread them, the more we see that Poe is less interested in the *commission* of crimes than in the *confession* to them. These are not so much stories of crime and detection as of crime and confession. For Poe, crime itself is not intellectually compelling. The actual business of murder is hurried through in both tales under discussion. In Poe's fullest exploration of the motiveless crime, "The Imp of the Perverse," the crime takes up almost no space at all. We don't know till we are two-thirds of the way through the largely essayistic text that we're reading a crime story at all.

Poe's murderers are not so much obsessive killers as obsessive *talkers*. Afflicted with what Poe calls in "The Black Cat" "the spirit of PERVERSENESS," their perversity lies not in their need to kill but in their need to tell. Thus, "The Imp of the Perverse" ends with the murderer's sense of safety: He's safe, he tells himself, "if I be not fool enough to make open confession" (1225). This thought is his undoing. "I well, too well understood that, to *think*, in my situation, was to be lost" (1225–6).

Concealment is ultimately unbearable for these killers, for whom secrets are like bodies buried alive, imprisoned souls seeking freedom. Thus, in "The Imp of the Perverse":

> For a moment, I experienced all the pangs of suffocation; I became blind, and deaf, and giddy; and then, some invisible fiend, I thought, struck me with his broad palm upon the back. The long-imprisoned secret burst forth from my soul.

Poe gives minute attention to the style of the released confession: "They say that I spoke with a distinct enunciation, but with marked emphasis and passionate hurry, as if in dread of interruption" (1226). Interruption would restore human separateness; these killers long for human transparency.

We have to consider other factors in making sense of the odd balance of crime and confession in these tales. Surely Poe had aesthetic reasons for minimizing the gore in his stories; as David Reynolds has pointed out, he wished to distance himself from popular practitioners of crime journalism, who relied on explicit horror to shock and titillate their readers.[9] It is Poe's corresponding emphasis on the act of confession that needs explanation. "The Tell-Tale Heart," "The Black Cat," and "The Imp" all record a confession – a *perverse* confession since the crimes would otherwise have been undetected. All three tales purport to be first-person narratives; they represent confessions within confessions – confessions to the second degree. These killers need to confess to the perverse act of having confessed. The fear of the criminals is not the fear of being caught, it is the fear of being *cut off*, of being misunderstood. Thus the narrator of "The Imp of the Perverse": "Had I not been thus prolix, you might either have misunderstood me altogether, or, with the rabble, have fancied me mad." Here, as in the other two tales, the claim to sanity is a response to the fear of being cut off from other people, of being "misunderstood altogether."

The speaker of "The Tell-Tale Heart," as we noted earlier, tells his story to convince his audience that he is not mad, not cut off from other people. The tale-telling heart is finally the narrator's own, for this is a tale about the need to communicate, the fear of being cut off, of becoming incommunicado. The narrator of "The

Black Cat" writes: "Yet, mad am I not.... But to-morrow I die, and today I would unburthen my soul. My immediate purpose is to place before the world, plainly, succinctly ... a series of mere household events." Communication, for these speakers, is itself a kind of salvation.

With this fear of isolation in mind, we can begin to make sense of what drives these killers crazy. The features these men can't stand are uncannily inexpressive: the eye with the hideous "film" or "veil" over it; the missing eye of the cats; the black fur. Similarly, the meaning of the ever-present walls in these stories is easily decoded. They represent the fantasy of being immured in one's own body, with the voice suffocated inside, the tale-telling heart silenced. Poe is quite explicit in "The Black Cat" when he says that the wall "fell bodily."

What of the beds that recur in so many of Poe's tales? We see immediately the attraction of beds as the site of many interrelated activities: sleep and dreaming; making love and conceiving children; dying. It is astonishing how many of Poe's stories centrally involve beds and bedrooms. In "The Imp" the victim is murdered by a poisoned candle while reading in bed; a bed is the means of escape in the Rue Morgue murders; and there are many tales – "Ligeia" especially – in which a woman lies on her deathbed.

Beds figure more prominently still in "The Tell-Tale Heart" and "The Black Cat." In the earlier story the killer, after a week of watching the old man asleep in bed, uses the bed itself as a murder weapon. It is not clear exactly how this is done, and this very lack of clarity makes Poe's choice of the bed more emphatic; he's willing to sacrifice verisimilitude – why not a knife or a noose? – in order to stress the meanings associated with the bed. Here is the description of the murder:

> He shrieked once – once only. In an instant I dragged him to the floor, and pulled the heavy bed over him. I then smiled gaily, to find the deed so far done. But, for many minutes, the heart beat on with a muffled sound. This, however, did not vex me; it would not be heard through the wall. At length it ceased. The old man was dead. I removed the bed and examined the corpse. Yes, he was stone, stone dead. I placed my hand upon the heart and held it there many minutes. There was no pulsation. He was stone dead. His eye would trouble me no more. (795–6)

Again the wall is clearly enough a stand-in for the body: "it would not be heard through the wall." But the bed also seems closely related to the body – Poe even appears to be playing on the similar sounds of the two words. The link of bed and dead body is clear enough in the sentence: "I removed the bed and examined the corpse."

Why should the bed be the murder weapon? Why not something more keyed to the filmed and infuriating eye? The answer, I think, is that whereas the bed resumes meanings associated with the body and its dissolution, it also draws on meanings linked to sexuality. The relationship between killer and victim in "The Tell-Tale Heart" is never specified, but we are told that the killer "loved the old man." The relation between killer and victim is similarly oblique in "The Imp of the Perverse," though we learn, in passing, that the killer inherits the victim's money.

Only in "The Black Cat" are these themes of intimacy and violence explored. We find ourselves amid walls and beds again after the killer's perverse act of hanging his cat – after he has "hung it *because* I knew that it had loved me, and *because* I felt it had given me no reason of offense." The following night the killer awakes to find "The curtains of my bed were in flames." When he returns to the ruins of the house he finds the following scene:

> The walls, with one exception, had fallen in. This exception was found in a compartment wall, not very thick, which stood about the middle of the house, and against which had rested the head of my bed. (853)

A crowd has assembled around this wall: "I approached and saw, as if graven in *bas relief* upon the white surface, the figure of a gigantic *cat*." The word "graven" is a brilliant stroke, for this is the cat's grave as well as his engraved monument. Poe is again – as with the pen/pen-knife and the poisoned reading candle – associating the violence of writing with the violence he is describing. Similarly, the "head of the bed" reminds us of the relation between bed and body.

Many critics have seen in this tale a close link between the cat and the wife, but this seems to me to place too much emphasis on marriage for at least two reasons. First, Poe is interested more in the issue of access to other minds – "hung it because *I knew* that it had loved me, and because *I felt* it had given me no reason of offense" [my emphasis] – and second, Poe is as interested in our access to the minds of cats as to the minds of people. (This is as good a place as any to acknowledge that I am leaving out two aspects of the narrative that are of obvious importance to a full reading of "The Black Cat" but are tangential to the themes of this essay: the issue of alcohol abuse and the issue of violence against women.)

The evidence for the second point lies in such essays as "Instinct vs Reason – A Black Cat," in which Poe speculates about the inner life of cats. After describing in some detail how his cat has mastered the art of opening the complicated latch of a door, he concludes that "The line which demarcates the instinct of the brute creation from the boasted reason of man, is, beyond doubt, of the most shadowy and unsatisfactory character" (477). Poe's meditations bear a surprising similarity to some of Wittgenstein's regarding the difference between animal thinking and that of humans. "Why can't a dog simulate pain?" asks Wittgenstein. "Is he too honest?" (250) Both writers speculate on how animals regard the future; Wittgenstein asks why we have difficulty imagining a hopeful animal ("And why not?" [174]), whereas Poe claims that the way his cat negotiates, step by step, the act of opening the latch demonstrates almost prophetic powers.

We are more interested, however, in the other focus of Poe's concern: our access to other (human) minds. "Unmotivated treachery, for the mere intent of injury, and self violence are," according to Allen Tate, "Poe's obsessive subjects."[10] This seems to me partly an oversimplification and partly wrong. Poe's killers do have motives, but these motives remain concealed from the killers. In the space remaining in this essay, I want to specify the link in Poe's tales between the profession of love and the need to confess. Both arise from what Frost, in our epigraph, called "the fear of Man – the fear that men won't understand us and we shall be cut off from them."

We need to understand what the teller/killer of "The Tell-Tale Heart" is really telling us when he claims that "Object there was none. Passion there was none. I loved the old man." He is, despite himself, providing both object (or motive) and passion. It is precisely his love for the old man that makes him kill, just as the man's love for the cat – "hung it *because* I knew that it had loved me" – prompts the murder of the cat and, presumably, the wife as well. At this point I must acknowledge the work of the philosopher Stanley Cavell in relation to the nature of Shakespearean tragedy. In plays like *Othello* and *King Lear* Cavell finds a repeated pattern of what he calls "the avoidance of love." Tragedy results from the burden that Lear and Othello find imposed by the love of others. In some sketchy and speculative remarks about Poe's "The Black Cat" and "The Imp of the Perverse," Cavell invites us to look for "some relation between the wish to be loved and the fear of it."[11]

The man we encounter in "The Black Cat" seems (and I am not claiming this is necessarily Cavell's view) to find the devotion of others repulsive. When the second cat follows the narrator home, he finds that "its evident fondness for myself rather disgusted and annoyed."

> With my aversion to this cat, however, its partiality for myself seemed to increase. It followed my footsteps with a pertinacity which it would be difficult to make the reader comprehend. Whenever I sat, it would crouch beneath my chair, or spring upon my knees, covering me with its loathsome caresses. (855)

Even in his dreams he finds the cat with him, and awakens "to find the hot breath of the thing upon my face, and its vast weight ...incumbent eternally upon my heart!" Our suspicion that Poe wishes, with the word "incumbent," to remind us of the sexual attentions of the mythical *incubus* and its counterpart the *succubus* is confirmed in the sentence immediately following: "Beneath the pressure of torments such as these, the feeble remnant of the good within me *succumbed.*"

It is another act of unbearable intimacy – when cat and wife insist on "accompanying" him into the cellar, and the cat follows him down "the steep stairs" so closely that it "exasperated me to madness" (856) – that incites the man to kill his two closest companions. We don't need Freud to point out the erotic connotations of steep stairs in dreams to feel that this man finds intimacy intolerable.

41

What Poe is giving voice to in these murders is the second fear Frost names: "the fear that we shan't prove worthy in the eyes of someone who knows us at least as well as we know ourselves." Frost calls this the fear of God, but it could as well be called the fear of Love. Here I am reminded of the German poet Rainer Maria Rilke's extraordinary reading of the parable of the Prodigal Son. Rilke interprets this tale of another once-tender man who flees into intemperance as "the legend of a man who didn't want to be loved." The picture Rilke paints is remarkably like the speaker in "The Black Cat." Here is Poe:

> From my infancy I was noted for the docility and humanity of my disposition. My tenderness of heart was even so conspicuous as to make me the jest of my companions. I was especially fond of animals. (850)

And here is Rilke:

> When he was a child, everyone in the house loved him. He grew up not knowing it could be any other way and got used to their tenderness, when he was a child.[12]

Both Poe's narrator and Rilke's prodigal come to find this intimacy unbearable. Rilke:

> He wouldn't have been able to say it, but when he spent the whole day roaming around outside and didn't even want to have the dogs with him, it was because they too loved him; because in their eyes he could see observation and sympathy, expectation, concern; because in their presence too he couldn't do anything without giving pleasure or pain.

The son's flight is from what he perceives as the prison of love – the way it defines and confines us.

> The dogs, in whom expectation had been growing all day long, ran through the hedges and drove you together into the one they recognized. And the house did the rest. Once you walked in to its full smell, most matters were already decided. A few details might still be changed; but on the whole you were already the person they thought you were; the person for whom they had long ago fashioned a life, out of his small past and their own desires; the creature belonging to them all, who stood day and night under the influence of their love.

Both Poe and Rilke (who would have known Poe's works through Baudelaire's essays and translations if through no more direct way) find in the very walls of the house and the eyes of pets the confining nature of domestic life, of what Poe calls "mere household events." If there is salvation for Rilke's prodigal in learning to love, and in accepting, eventually, God's love, there is none for Poe's murderers. As Allen Tate remarked, "He has neither Purgatory nor Heaven."[13] Poe's narratives can be read as cautionary tales – "Go thou and do otherwise" – but rightly read their warning is more complex. Poe seems, like Frost, to be saying: These fears are always with us – the fear of love and the fear of isolation. Taken to extremes, they both lead to disaster: One cat avoids us and is blinded, another cat follows us and is killed. To live life is to steer a dangerous course between these extremes and there is no point at which the current widens. To declare oneself safe – as the imp of the perverse tempts us to do – is to be lost.

NOTES

1 Robert Frost, "Introduction" to Edwin Arlington Robinson, *King Jasper* (New York: Scribner's, 1935), p. vi.

2 *Collected Works of Edgar Allan Poe*, ed. Thomas Ollive Mabbott (Cambridge: Harvard University Press, 1978), p. 528. All future page references to this edition are indicated in parentheses in the text.

3 Richard Wilbur, "The House of Poe," in *Edgar Allan Poe: Modern Critical Views*, ed. Harold Bloom (New York: Chelsea House, 1985), pp. 51–69.

4 Harold Bloom, "Introduction," in *Edgar Allan Poe*, p. 8.

5 David S. Reynolds, *Beneath the American Renaissance: The Subversive Imagination in the Age of Emerson and Melville* (New York: Knopf, 1988), pp. 225–48.

6 Poe, *Essays and Reviews*, ed. G. R. Thompson (New York: Library of America, 1984), p. 1426.

7 Richard Wilbur, "Poe and the Art of Suggestion," in *Critical Essays on Edgar Allan Poe*, ed. Eric W. Carlson (Boston: G. K. Hall, 1987), p. 166.

8 Ludwig Wittgenstein, *Philosophical Investigations*, trans. G. E. M. Anscombe (New York: Macmillan, 1958). The numbers attached to this and later references to Wittgenstein refer not to pages but to numbered sections of the *Investigations*.

9 Reynolds remarks that "Poe... avoids repulsive accounts of violence or blood, shifting his attention to the crazed mind of the obsessed narrator. By removing us from the realm of horrid gore to that of diseased psychology, he rises above... tawdry sensationalism" (*Beneath the American Renaissance*, p. 232).

10 Allen Tate, "Our Cousin, Mr. Poe," in *Poe: A Collection of Critical Essays*, ed. Robert Regan (Englewood Cliffs, N.J.: Prentice-Hall, 1967), p. 46.

11 Stanley Cavell, *In Quest of the Ordinary* (Chicago: University of Chicago Press, 1990), p. 137. See also Cavell, *The Claim of Reason: Wittgenstein, Skepticism, Morality, and Tragedy* (Oxford: Oxford University Press, 1979), pp. 481–96.

12 Rainer Maria Rilke, *The Notebooks of Malte Laurids Brigge*, trans. Stephen Mitchell (New York: Random House, 1983), pp. 251–60.

13 Tate, "Our Cousin," p. 46.

3

The Perverse Strategy in "The Fall of the House of Usher"

LOUISE J. KAPLAN

> The root of all evil is that we all want this spiritual gratification, this flow, this apparent heightening of life, this knowledge, this valley of many-colored grass, even grass and light prismatically decomposed, giving ecstasy. We want all this *without resistance.* We want it continually. And this is the root of all evil in us.
>
> —D.H. Lawrence, "Edgar Allan Poe" [1]

EDGAR Allan Poe was a dissembler, a hoaxter, a liar, an impostor, and plagiarizer. He was secretive about his true identity and frequently masqueraded under one of several aliases. Deception and mystification were Poe's stock-in-trade. Nevertheless, about some things we take him at his word. He truly was, as he boasted, a master of perversion, that most deceptive of mental strategies. We have only to recall his persistent and active pursuit of mental and physical self-destruction – the drinking, his habits of provocative and violent argumentation, the alienation of his guardian and other authority figures who might otherwise have given him support, the pedophilic-incestuous undercurrents of his marriage. Then there is the miasma surrounding his death – was it the outcome of one of his provocations, or disease, alcoholism, suicide, dementia? In living his life and even in his manner of negotiating death, Poe was a captive of the imp of perversity. But with Art as his shield, the realms of perversity became a haven for his troubled soul. He left to posterity a documentation of the spirit of the imp who held him enthralled.

In "The Imp of the Perverse," Poe explained the logic beneath the apparent unreasonableness of this "innate and primitive principle of human action" which prompts us to act solely "for the reason that we should *not.*" Whereas all other faculties and impulses of the human soul could be seen as expressions of the human need for self-preservation, in the instance of perversity "the desire to be well is not only not aroused, but a strongly antagonistical sentiment exists." [2]

With that cagey "not only not," Poe renders precisely the double negative duplicity of the perverse strategy. From a psychoanalytic perspective, perversion is not only not simply (or necessarily) an aberration of the sexual life, or merely some irresistible impulse to perform an act insidious to the moral order. Perversion is a complex strategy of mind, with its unique principles for regulating the negotiations between Desire and Authority. To achieve its aims, the perverse strategy employs mechanisms of mystification, concealment, and illusion, devices characteristic of the tales of Edgar Allan Poe. The perverse strategy is, as Poe might have put it, a faculty of the human soul.

Among the elements of the perverse strategy that we will encounter in "The Fall of the House of Usher" are certain literary devices aimed at revealing truth by way of concealment. Poe believed that truly imaginative literature locates its deepest meaning in an *under*current. The surfaces of his tales are always deceptions. Initiated readers of Poe relish the deceptions and anticipate having to pore diligently over his texts to detect the embedded secrets. The tale of Usher is shrouded in mystifying atmospheres, references to obscure texts, and hints of enigmatic events. Poe's impish invitation to detect hidden meanings in one place distracts the reader from other crucial events going on behind the scenes. Whatever enigmas Poe brings into focus in "The Fall of the House of Usher," there are always the shadows of the unseen, the uncanny, the unknowable, implications of some darker secret that is being kept from us.

Indeed, to apprehend the ambiguities in "The Fall of the House of Usher" a reader must possess the analytical skills of a good detective. A few years after his account of the fall of Usher, Poe invented the detective story and created the prototypical detective, Monsieur C. Auguste Dupin. Dupin is "fond of enigmas, of conundrums, of hieroglyphics; exhibiting in his solutions of each a degree of *acumen* which appears to the ordinary apprehension praeternatural" (528). Poe cautions, a person of *mere* ingenuity may be incapable of analysis. Despite his lavish (and duplicitous) displays of scientific reasoning, Dupin arrives at his solutions by way of imaginative leaps and an uncanny attunement with the mind of the criminal. Roderick Usher is at once an imaginative artist and a criminal. Although a certain fondness for enigmas is necessary to appreciate "The Fall of the House of Usher," it is our grasp of the perverse strategy that provides an attunement with Usher's troubled soul.

Poe was not above employing puzzles and enigmas as seductions into the mere ingenuity he disdained. In the history of Poe criticism, these seductions have been all too successful. For example, those not wise to the diversionary tactics of the imp have attributed Poe's facility with the logic of perversity to the primal traumas of his infancy and early childhood. When Poe was about eighteen months old, his alcoholic father abandoned the family. Shortly thereafter, Edgar witnessed the sickness, decay, and death of his mother. He became an orphan and his sister and brother disappeared. Poe's tales are convincing depictions of the castrations, separations, abandonments, and annihilations that constitute the typical anxieties of childhood, anxieties that in Poe's case must have reached overwhelming and therefore traumatic proportions. Poe's portrayals of body mutilations, smotherings, drownings, entombments of the living, the wasting away and rotting away of bodies, situations emptied of human dialogue, are calculated to re-evoke in the reader the archaic fears of childhood. It would not be farfetched to conjecture that Poe embraced these themes as a way of mastering the passively suffered traumas of his childhood.

We miss the point of all this, however, if we reduce "The Fall of the House of Usher" to Poe's personal traumas or his inclinations to sexual aberration and violence. Instead, as I said, I will take Poe at his word. I will use the tale of Usher as a demonstration of Poe's mastery of the perverse strategy, with its mystifications and concealments, its ambiguous relationship to the moral order, its pretense of a fundamental antagonism to representational reality. As I assess the currents and undercurrents of "The Fall of the House of Usher," my interpretations of the moral and aesthetic plights of the artist protagonist, Roderick Usher, will be guided by the principles of the perverse strategy. Nevertheless, in this tale, where specters of incest and necrophilia hover in the background, perversion in its narrower and customary sense – as sexual aberration – will inform my concluding interpretations.

47

First printed in 1839 in *Burton's Magazine*, "The Fall of the House of Usher" was six years later included in Poe's *Tales of the Grotesque and Arabesque*. The very terms Poe chose to describe his tales are expressive of the confusions between the real and the imaginary, the animate and the inanimate that characterize the perverse strategy. Arabesque is derived from Arabian and Moorish art and refers to an elaborate design in which highly stylized human and animal figures are embedded among intertwined branches, foliage, and fanciful scrollwork. Crucial to the complexity of the artistic design of "The Fall of the House of Usher," is the way in which Usher's person and fate are intertwined with the decaying foliage and crumbling ornate architectural scrollwork of his House. We are repeatedly reminded of the sentience of nonliving matter and the decay of living matter back into nonbeing. Grotesque is an ornamental style of antiquity, which one of Poe's lesser known critics has described as "something playfully gay and carelessly fantastic but also something ominous and sinister, in the face of a world in which the realm of inanimate things are no longer separated from those of plants, animals and human beings and where the laws of statics, symmetry, and proportion are no longer valid."[3] "The Fall of the House of Usher" depends for its emotional effects on the dissolving of the boundaries between the inanimate and animate realms and the breaking down of the laws of everyday reality. Though this tale could hardly be recommended for its playful gaiety, the reader is playfully engaged in solving mysteries, protected until the very end from the full knowledge of the ominous and sinister events going on behind the scenes.

The tale's epigraph from De Béranger warns of a potential dissolution of the borders between illusion and reality. We learn at once that the heart of the artist, Roderick Usher, is like a lute that resonates to all that touches it:

> Son coeur est un luth suspendu:
> Sitôt qu'on le touche il résonne. (397)

Poe, the creator of Roderick Usher, does not lose his boundaries. Through the trickery, call it technique, of mystification and enigma, Poe achieves the deceptions, call them illusions, that comprise his artistic strategy. In "The Fall of the House of Usher" various illusory devices are employed to preserve the borders of the moral order, even as they mischievously render a picture of moral disintegration. The House of Usher decays, crumbles, and falls into oblivion but it does so in a manner eminently lawful and orderly. The tale is partitioned, one could say precisely measured, into three equal and distinct acts. The events take place within a month, beginning with the desolation and gloom surrounding the narrator's approach to the House and ending with the abrupt, noisy, and violent circumstances of his departure.

Act One introduces the characters, depicts the eerie effect the House of Usher has on its viewers and inhabitants, and apprises us of Roderick's family background and the general nature of his illness. The first character we meet is the narrator, who, in response to an agitated letter from his childhood companion Roderick Usher, has set off on a journey to his House. He has certain misgivings and the closer he comes to the House the more these misgivings increase. Nevertheless he hopes that his presence will help alleviate his old friend's maladies – a mysterious bodily illness accompanied by an oppressive mental disorder. We learn that Roderick and his sister, Lady Madeline, are the last of the Ushers, a family known for its inbreeding and deficiency ''of collateral issue'' as well as for its unassuming deeds of charity and devotion to the intricacies of musical science. As the narrator moves through numerous, winding passageways to the studio of his friend, he encounters a valet with a stealthy step and the Usher family physician, whose expression of ''low cunning and perplexity'' further enhances the mood of suspicion, gloom, and FEAR that envelops the Usher mansion. Save for the peculiar dialogues between the narrator and Roderick, the universe of ordinary human dialogue is notable for its absence. Aside from the brief appearances of the valet and physician the staff of the mansion is invisible and uncannily silent. Madeline utters not one word. But the canny dialogue of detection between Poe and his reader is vibrant.

Roderick tells the narrator that his sufferings stem from a disorder of the senses: He is oppressed by every odor, even of flowers. His tastebuds can endure only the most insipid food; his skin can tolerate only garments of the slightest texture; his eyes are tortured by the faintest of lights, and save for the tones from his own stringed instruments, every sound inspires Roderick with horror. Existence itself is a torment for Roderick. He lives with the dread that this pitiable condition of his senses will eventually lead him to "abandon life and reason together, in some struggle with the grim phantasm, FEAR." He is possessed by a superstition that the form and substance of the House itself, the very sentience of the stones and foliage, have obtained a power over his spirit. Finally Roderick hints that his gloom could be attributable to the severe and lengthy illness of his beloved sister, "his sole companion for long years – his last and only relative on earth" (404). As Roderick utters these words, Lady Madeline passes through a remote corner of his large studio and vanishes.

In Act Two the narrator quickly discovers the futility of "cheering a mind from which darkness, as if an inherent positive quality, poured forth upon all objects of the moral and physical universe, in one unceasing radiation of gloom" (405). Nevertheless he does not give up on his mission of salvation. He spends several days alone with Roderick, reading from the esoteric texts in his library, watching him paint, listening to the wild improvised dirges his friend plucks from his speaking guitar. Most of this act is given over to detailed descriptions of Roderick's paintings, music, and poetry. It concludes with the "death" of Madeline and her entombment in a vault at the bottommost reaches of the House of Usher. As the narrator and Roderick go about the preparations for Madeline's burial, the reader learns that she is Roderick's *twin* sister, and also the disquieting fact that her features still glow from the blush of life. Immediately following Madeline's entombment, Roderick's mental condition deteriorates and the narrator becomes infected with his friend's fantastic imaginings and superstitions.

Act Three takes place on a stormy night about a week after the entombment of Lady Madeline. Usher comes to the narrator's room in a state of "mad hilarity" and hysteria. In an attempt to calm him, the narrator reads aloud from the tale of the "Mad Trist." The sounds described in this tale are soon echoed by the sounds of Madeline escaping from her tomb. Roderick exclaims, *"We have put her living in the tomb!"* Madeline appears in the doorway, and in her final death agonies, falls inward on her brother, bearing him "to the floor a corpse, and a victim to the terrors he had anticipated" (417). The narrator flees in terror from the chamber and from the mansion. He looks back to see the mighty walls of the House of Usher burst asunder and fall into a dank tarn that closes over its fragments.

With sin and violence so much in the foreground of Poe's tales, we are apt to forget that they are as much about the structures of reason and moral order as they are about the forces that undermine those structures, causing them to totter and collapse in on themselves as they do in "The Fall of the House of Usher." The protagonist, Roderick Usher, is an artist and the central conflicts concern the artist's ambiguous relation to the moral order. In a tale of an artist, matters of Art cannot be incidental. The decay and eventual fall of the House of Usher are inextricably linked to the crumbling away of the borders between reality and illusion in Roderick's art. The lengthy descriptions of his paintings, musical performances, and poetry are crucial to the *under*currents of "The Fall of the House of Usher," and to the affinities between creativity and perversion. Poe's tale of the life and death of the artist, Roderick Usher, depicts the creative processes that enabled Usher's art along with the moral nihilism his art was striving to regulate and contain.

In his essay "The Poetic Principle" Poe stated that the highest art is to be "found in *an elevating excitement of the Soul* − quite independent of that passion which is the intoxication of the Heart − or that Truth which is the satisfaction of the Reason."[4] Richard Wilbur, in "The House of Poe," distinguished between Poe's proclaimed aesthetic of repudiating the human and earthly in favor of *poésie pure* − the visionary uncontaminated by passion, the imaginative unconstrained by logic or reason − and his more down-to-earth literary method of posing moral riddles in the form of prose allegories. Wilbur deplored the aesthetic expressed by the visionary Poe in his essays on music and poetry, but honored the method employed by the logical Poe in allegories such as "William Wilson," "Ligeia," "MS. Found in a Bottle," and "The Fall of the House of Usher." About the allegories, Wilbur says:

In them, Poe broke wholly new ground and they remain the best things of their kind in our literature. Poe's mind may have been a strange one; yet all minds are alike in their general structure; therefore we can understand him, and I think that he will have something to say to us as long as there is civil war in the palaces of men's minds.[5]

Whereas Poe's aesthetic entails a conscious undermining of reality and authority in order to attain the rhythms of a pure visionary art, his prose allegories derive their effects from the vibrancy of the negotiations between Desire and Authority. In other words, "the civil war" in the palace of the mind acts as a resistance to the wish for pure gratification. In the absence of such resistance, without moral conflict, the aesthetic of *poésie pure* is the equivalent of a moral nihilism.

Analogously, we might say that sexual aberration with its conscious claim for unrestrained gratification is the aesthetic of perversion, whereas the perverse strategy is an unconscious method that regulates the life of Desire. In contrast to the sexual aberrations which have, as a conscious aim, an undermining of Authority, the strategy of perversion is an attempt to preserve the moral order. Paradoxically then, the interests of the moral order – what some psychoanalysts call "ego and superego" and others "the symbolic order" and still others "the structures of language" – are served by the perverse strategy. In a canny duplicity, the perverse strategy achieves its moral aims by permitting a token expression to Sin and even to the torments, anxieties, melancholia, and violence that accompany moral disorder. As in all Poe's allegories, in the tale of Usher these frightful states of mind are given a due measure of expression – but all regulated and contained within the boundaries of art.

Like Usher, who evinces a fundamental antagonism to earthly reality in favor of imaginative purity, Poe spurned realistic descriptions and representational devices in favor of setting tones and creating moods that would engender abnormal states of mind. He wanted to shake readers loose from the moorings of everyday earthly life so their imaginations might be freed; so they might suspend disbelief and accept as true something patently untrue. In "The Fall of the House of Usher" Poe engenders illusion and yet preserves a sense of reality; he replaces what otherwise might be a feeling of overwhelming dread with playful shudders, thrills, excitements. Literary devices that confound what is true by masking it with the untrue, or substitute pleasurable emotions for painful ones, are analogous to fetishism, the paradigmatic instance of the perverse strategy.

Imposturing, petty lies, plagiarism, in fact, any act, object, thought, or artistic device that wards off the perception of an unwelcome or unbearable reality and substitutes instead perceptions that facilitate ambiguity and illusion can be thought of as the equivalent of a fetish.

In sexual fetishism, for example, a fetish – a garter belt, boot, slipper, whip, corset, negligee – is employed to counteract the unwelcome and frightening reality of a woman's actual body and to engender the illusion of a phallic woman, a person who is female but whose genitals nevertheless are identical to those of a male. This act of fetishizing a woman's body protects the fetishist from the anxious reality of the differences between the sexes. However, this shield against the "real" reality, though it enhances an illusion that rescues the capacity for sexual intercourse, can only be accomplished through a dehumanization and deanimation of the sexual partner. Thus in fetishism an experiencing, breathing body is deadened, entombed as it were, like the still blushing, earthly body of Madeline Usher, in the realm of the living dead. My concluding interpretations will stress how Roderick Usher's break with the moral order is connected with his need to repudiate the reality of Madeline's sexuality. For now I am using the model of fetishism to show how Roderick Usher's artistic devices contrasted with those of his creator, Edgar Allan Poe. In his quest for a pure aesthetic, Usher eventually loses his connection with the moral order. Poe never does.

The fetishist's apparent antagonism to reality is not so absolute and fundamental as it first appears. Nor is Poe so wholeheartedly committed to the aesthetic of pure Supernal Beauty he promulgates in "The Poetic Principle." Poe demonstrates his divided loyalties by always acknowledging the principles of reason and logic even as he creates an atmosphere of illusion and mystification. With his fetishistic devices, the fetishist is *disavowing* the reality of differences between the sexes, while simultaneously *avowing* that reality. His fears engender an illusion of identity between the sexes. The passions of his heart, his earthly sexual desires, are an acknowledgment of the sexual difference. With one part of his mind working to conceal differences, another part is still aware of reality. There is what is called in psychoanalysis "a split in the ego," a fissure or rupture in the mind, but not a full departure from the world of reality. The fetishist is not a madman who simply denies or *repudiates* reality, as Roderick Usher eventually does. Nor is he one of your standard neurotics, like perhaps the narrator of Poe's tale, who *represses* any knowledge that frightens or humiliates him.

In the life of Edgar Allan Poe, artistic creation served as a version of disavowal, a kind of fetishistic device that enabled him to conceal and yet still reveal the unbearable secrets and phantoms that haunted his mind. Moreover, the lies, tricks, conundrums, enigmas, and mystifications characteristic of Poe's tales function like a fetish. In "The Fall of the House of Usher," various artistic media and art objects are employed in a fashion analogous to a fetish. Like translucent veils placed between the reader and what would otherwise be a full knowledge of some dark, unwelcome reality, the ambiguity and illusory quality of Roderick's works of art serve to distract and conceal. Yet, and this is the heart of Poe's artistic strategy, these same art objects simultaneously reveal in a symbolic form what would be too unbearable to acknowledge directly. While readers are kept busy detecting the enigmas suggested by Roderick's art (and the esoteric books in his library), Lady Madeline is being de-animated, buried alive, entombed in the land of the living dead. Yet, just as an analysis of the symbolic structure of a sexual fetish would tell us about the unconscious mental life of the fetishist, so the symbolic structure of Roderick's art reveals his unconscious forbidden wishes.

Poe tells us that Usher's heart is like a lute that can only quiver helplessly and passively to the throbs of nature. Usher himself laments that his body, his very soul is being pervaded by the atmosphere of his house, but this complaint to the narrator may very well be a vast deception, a clever subterfuge. In Usher's ascetic avoidance of sensuous earthly pleasures is he not, in fact, inviting a merger with spirits, phantoms, foliage, stones, atmospheres?

Would our earthbound narrator ever dare such risky excitements of the soul?

When the House of Usher first comes into sight, the narrator finds it impossible to erect any cover of illusion between the decaying images before his eyes and his soul. In fact the very opposite occurs. There is "a hideous dropping off of the veil." The narrator experiences "an iciness, a sinking, a sickening of the heart – an unredeemed dreariness of thought which no goading of the imagination could torture into aught of the sublime" (397).

Though the narrator strives to impress us with his altruism and therapeutic zeal, one suspects that he has responded to Roderick's summons in order to gratify his personal quest for the sublime. With a mental contrivance that merely impersonates Art, the narrator turns his eyes away from the awe inspiring spectacle of the House and interposes an illusory arrangement of its features. He stops before a tarn that reflects the inverted image of the house with its grey and ghastly foliage and "vacant and eyelike windows." His gaze into the tarn does not, however, entirely dispel his anxiety; it transforms anxiety into a more tolerable fear. Indeed, the new visual arrangement brings "a shudder even more thrilling than before," but thrilling is a distance from the overwhelming melancholy and sinister import of the actual images. Poe's "thrilling" is all the seduction his readers require. We will not be disappointed. We are in for a bit of excitement. Our playful quivering apprehension will capture the essence of some terrible anxiety and shield us from the displeasure and terror we might otherwise experience. A roller coaster ride may scare us to death, but we gladly defy death for the elation of the thrills it promises. We enter the illusion willingly, even daringly, assured that we are not actually going to be smashed to pieces and die. In the tale of Usher, elated feelings of risk and excitement replace the mental sufferings – anxiety, depression, madness – we might otherwise experience if we were to actually feel as Roderick feels.

Poe invites us to resonate with Roderick's "FEAR." The thrilling 'ale the narrator relates will be the artifice that shields the reader 'm Roderick's unbearable moral plights. Poe, the artist, renders 'e that both reveals and conceals the torments of a soul that 'e boundaries of the symbolic order.

The logical Poe sides with truth and reason, but from the point of view of the visionary Poe, Roderick's release from reason and descent into madness is an act of artistic courage. The narrator who tells Usher's tale in his earnest, measured, reasonable way, is a coward who flirts with the dangerous process of Art and then furtively shrinks into the shadows of normality.

At each step of the way, from the moment the narrator has the inspiration to rearrange the particulars of the scene by inverting them, Art is evoked to conceal yet reveal the gradual but inexorable dissolution of Roderick's tie to the world of ordinary mortals. The art forms, poetry, painting, music, and even the obscure scholarly texts on the sentience of the inanimate world, books which "had formed no small portion of the mental existence of the invalid" (408), express and reflect Roderick's plight, while by their continued connection to the symbolic order, they veil the horrors they express. As the last of his futile efforts to protect Roderick from the terrors encroaching on his mind and consuming his soul, the narrator reads aloud from the "Mad Trist," a vulgar grotesque by Sir Launcelot Canning. In this choice, the narrator confesses to an ingenuous duplicity: "I had called it a favorite of Usher's more in sad jest than in earnest; for, in truth, there is little in its uncouth and unimaginative prolixity which could have had interest for the lofty and spiritual ideality of my friend" (413). The subtly "thrilling" shudders of Poe's "The Fall of the House of Usher" rouse the imagination and we accept as real and actual the ghastly sounds of Madeline Usher clawing her way out of her tomb. However, the blatant clangings and rattlings of the merely fanciful "Mad Trist" are so cheaply obtained as to be laughable.

Roderick's art, his music, his paintings, his poetry strive for aesthetic purity. Roderick is willing to risk his soul for Art. His bodily asceticism serves as a protection against earthly human desires. With his art, Roderick seems to be deliberately negating the palpable representational world. This negation of tangible reality is Roderick's effort to achieve a more intimate attunement with nature and even go so far as to dissolve his being in the sentience of nonliving matter. Only with this painful and frightening dissolution of the boundaries of the self can Roderick free his imagination and create new art forms. As D. H. Lawrence said in his essay on Poe, "old things need to die and disintegrate . . . before anything else can come to pass. . . . Man must be stripped even of himself. And it is a painful, sometimes a ghastly, process."[6]

A contemporary reader might well wonder if Roderick did not invent abstract expressionism. The sounds and images created by Roderick overpower the ordinary, definitive, and concrete realities, replacing them with perceptions that facilitate ambiguity and illusion. "An excited and highly distempered ideality threw a sulphureous lustre over all." Even when his images lean on reality, Roderick distorts that reality beyond any ordinary recognition. An example is his "singular perversion and amplification of the wild air of the last waltz of Von Weber" (405).

The narrator is enthralled as he watches Roderick's paintings grow "touch by touch into vaguenesses." The more abstract and ambiguous they become "the more thrillingly" the narrator shudders. Of these "phantasmagoric conceptions" the narrator recalls one painting that was "not so rigidly of the spirit of abstraction." The imagery was just sufficiently representational to allow the narrator to "shadow forth, although feebly, in words," a description. The image the narrator recalls is the interior of an immensely long and rectangular vault that lay at an exceeding depth below the surface of the earth. Though no source of light is discernible, "a flood of intense rays rolled throughout, and bathed the whole in a ghastly and inappropriate splendor" (406). We later learn that this chiaroscuro image is a harbinger of Madeline's tomb.

Another of Roderick's productions is far less abstract and more obviously premonitory. With the advantage of hindsight, the narrator, now comfortably distant from the frightening events he relates, recollects the words of one of the ballads Roderick sang as he strummed his singing guitar. In its conventional phrasing and structure "The Haunted Palace" evidences a mind capable of the "collectedness and concentration" the narrator admires. When he wrote the ballad Roderick was still in command of the formal properties of poetry. His madness was still only incipient. Yet the words imply, at least to the conventional and cautious narrator, that Roderick is aware of the fate that awaits him. "In the under or mystic current of its meaning, I fancied that I perceived, and for the first time, a full consciousness on the part of Usher, of the tottering of his lofty reason upon her throne" (406).

Whereupon the narrator recites the verses of Usher's ballad, an abbreviated version of a poem written by Poe for another occasion and self-plagiarized to express the plight of Roderick Usher. Inevitably, the avid detectives who delight in fathoming Poe's deeper meanings note that all his mansions and buildings are structured like the human body, parts of the human body, or as layers or aspects of the mind. Often as not, the Usher mansion or the haunted palace of the mind in Roderick's ballad are cited as epitome and proof of this interpretation. The first four stanzas are said to represent a head, moreover a head with a lawful and orderly mind still capable of uttering words of authority; the flowing, glorious, golden banners are likened to hair, the windows through which wanderers might see "Spirits moving musically / To a lute's well-tunéd law" are likened to luminous eyes, the pearly and ruby doorway giving forth the wit and wisdom of the king is, of course, a mouth. The two concluding stanzas, which depict "red-litten windows" and "forms that move fantastically / To a discordant melody," are said to represent a sick and disordered mind. Like the narrator who is himself a missionary from the land of law and order, many of Poe's critics interpret "The Haunted Palace" as Poe's lament to the tottering of Roderick's mind, his loss of connection to the life of reason. Surely, however, there must be an undercurrent beneath the current so easily and ingeniously detected by our reasonable narrator.

Let us consider "The Haunted Palace" from the point of view of the artist, Roderick Usher, rather than from the perspective of the frightened traveler who turned aghast from the revelations of Usher's Art, running as fast as he could back to civilization with its clear boundaries between real and not real, animate and non-animate, to tell an orderly tale. For Usher, as for any imaginative artist, the lyrics of his ballad might be less a lament to lost reason and more a tribute to innocence and free imagination. In this light, the "glory that blushed and bloomed" and now will "smile no more" could be interpreted as the innocent soul of the child. The child is the king who utters wisely, whereas the adult, the moral authority who enforces the life of reason, depriving the child of his contact with the world of sensate flux, is the corrupt one. The ''evil things, in robes of sorrow'' that ''assailed the monarch's high estate'' are the forces of civilization.

Poe, like the poets he idealized to the point of plagiarism, envisioned childhood as a time of glorious innocence, an innocence betrayed by the laws of reason and morality. Childhood was discovered (some say invented) in the eighteenth century in response to the dehumanizing trends of the industrial revolution. By the nineteenth century, when artists began to see themselves as alienated beings trapped in a dehumanizing social world, the child became the symbol of free imagination and goodness. Blake and Wordsworth, and soon Dickens and Twain, were preoccupied with themes of childhood innocence. The image of the child was set in opposition to the prison of civilization. By peering into the soul of the child, the artist hoped to rediscover some divine state of selfhood. The artist looked to the child as the representation of that original True Self that was lost when man became a social being. Whatever is noble and pure and good about the human being could be found in the child, who, living freely in the world of sensate flux, a world uncorrupted by language and reason, is closest to the natural world, the realm of existence where soul and imagination flourish.

Clearly the narrator and Usher are at odds, not only in their attitudes to art but also in their moral values. The narrator is a conventional moralist, who even as he follows Usher into vaults and cellars and underground passages and thrills to the shudders they evoke, still clings desperately to the world of reality. Usher, on the other hand, has deliberately isolated himself from the world of earthly delights and from the moral order itself, in order to create visionary abstractions. The narrator, who has entered this heart of darkness on a mission of rescue, is frustrated by Usher's passive surrender to his illness. He suspects that Usher is nourishing the dark melancholy that he projected ''upon all objects of the moral and physical universe'' (405) as if it were a positive force. With a mind still fettered by the temporal, physical world that Usher has shaken off, the narrator cannot apprehend ''The Haunted Palace'' as anything other than a sign of Usher's descent into madness. Finally it is Usher who turns to the narrator, crying out "Madman." But who is the madman?

Recall that the perverse strategy encourages an illusory excitement that approximates madness in order to shield the mind against a more profound madness. To appreciate the nature of this other madness, let us return to the narrower meaning of perversion, perversion as sexual aberration.

Fetishism, in its literal, narrow sense enables sexual intercourse through a displacement of sexual desire away from the whole identity of a woman to some accessory or garment, some object ancillary to her being – a shoe or a garter belt. Why should a man be unable to experience sexual desire for a woman without the protection of a fetishistic device?

Until quite recently when psychoanalysts began to scrutinize the symbolic structure of the sexual fetish, the need to create a fetish was taken as presumable evidence of the castration anxiety evoked by the frightening vision of the absent and therefore castrated female genitals. It was assumed that there is something innately horrifying about the female body, something about her life-giving passages of sexuality and procreation that would inevitably bring to men's minds the stigmata of humiliation, degradation, mutilation, and death. However, this perennial theme of the female stigmata is now appreciated as a disguise, a cover-up we might say, for a man's secret and forbidden unconscious wishes – to merge with woman, to be her, to never leave the Garden of Eden of childhood where sacred mother and innocent child are united for eternity. In Eden the mother is pure and asexual. To acknowledge the mother's sexuality and her earthly desire is equivalent to a banishment from Eden. The fetish object conceals and disguises the sexual difference, thereby granting simultaneously an earthly passion of the Heart and the exalted spiritual wish to be reunited with the mother.

These currents of Poe's tale surface in the relation between Madeline and Roderick. Although much intervenes to intrigue and distract the reader of "The Fall of the House of Usher," the specter of incest is omnipresent from the beginning. We are told at once that the barely perceptible fissure down the center of the mansion and the decay of its stones are expressions of the deficiency "of collateral issue, and the consequent undeviating transmission from sire to son, of the patrimony with the name." In a tale heavy with ambiguities, Poe's words to describe the incestuous family background of Madeline and Roderick are ominously ambiguous:

> [T]he stem of the Usher race, all time-honored as it was, had put forth, at no period, any enduring branch; in other words, . . . the entire family lay in the direct line of descent, and had always, with very trifling and very temporary variation, so lain. (399)

Unless the twins, Madeline and Roderick, surrender to their earthly passions and commit incest, they are doomed to be the last of the Usher line. Was Roderick's asceticism, his avoidance of all bodily temptations, aimed at avoiding incest? Or did he endure the ghastly process of self-disintegration in order to create new forms of art? D. H. Lawrence introduces his essay on Poe by saluting the forces of dissolution, disintegration, and death, declaring them vital to the life of free imagination. However, Lawrence recognized that as much as "The Fall of the House of Usher" is about the risky ecstasies of a genuine artistic sensibility, it is also a tale of love. This is where the moral ambiguities lie. The spiritual ecstasy that is essential to Roderick's creativity becomes a force of evil in his love for Madeline. To put these issues another way: The tale of love in "The Fall of the House of Usher" reveals the terrible consequences of an aesthetic of pure gratification, when that aesthetic no longer engages the resistance of the moral order.

Lawrence warned, "There is a limit to love." He grasped precisely the force of evil in the spiritual bond between the two last survivors of the House of Usher. In sensual love, there is never a complete fusion or merger. The boundaries between self and other never completely dissolve. In spiritual love, however, the lovers vibrate in unison and their beings merge. In the vibrating, spiritual love between Madeline and Roderick:

> the mystery of the recognition of *otherness* fails, [and] the longing for identification with the beloved becomes a lust. And it is this longing for identification, utter merging, which is at the base of the incest problem. . . . In the family, the natural vibration is most nearly in unison. With a stranger, there is greater resistance. Incest is the getting of gratification and the avoiding of resistance.[7]

61

Both Madeline and Roderick are dying of asceticism, of their mutual need to banish every sign of sensuality or earthly desire. Madeline's physical presence is a reminder to Roderick of his earthly passions. She is slowly wasting away, but her skin still blushes with the blood of life. In light of Roderick's conflicted feelings toward his sister, I would interpret "The Haunted Palace" as an expression of his wish to restore the spirituality of his love for Madeline. The contrasting images in this ballad represent two images of Madeline: the Madeline of childhood in her days of glorious innocence, and the bloody, lewd Madeline, the Madeline of sexual desire and the wild intoxications of the Heart.

Childhood innocence is about the life of Desire before the knowledge of female sexuality and the male-female sexual difference. It is the oedipal child, the child who must leave the world of sensate flux and free imagination and enter the symbolic order with its rules of language, reason, and morality, who resurrects the earlier uncomplicated infantile wish to merge with the mother, now as a defense against the knowledge of the irrevocable and irreversible differences between the sexes. With a full acknowledgment of these differences would come the painful acknowledgment that the life of Desire can never be pure. Once the child enters the moral order, the elevating excitements of the Soul cannot exist independently of earthly passions and the intoxications of the Heart – or the Truth of Reason.

Asceticism, the total avoidance of sensual pleasure, is an avoidance of the complex negotiations between Desire and Authority. When the effort to banish passion through asceticism fails, as eventually it must, there is either a fulfillment of a forbidden sexual desire or something worse – the madness of total emotional surrender to the other and a loss of identity.

Emotional surrender entails a total dissolution of the boundaries between the real and the not real. Thus, in ridding himself of the intoxications of the Heart, the passions of incestuous desire, Roderick is attempting a more insidious violation of the moral order. For, as Lawrence detected, latent in the undercurrent of an apparent sexual incestuous wish is the wish for a spiritual merger with the other. Roderick's deepest and most frightening wish is to merge with Madeline, to be eternally united with her in some smooth womblike utopia where the rough realities of earthly existence would no longer disturb his peace. Our most profound fears are always a reflection of our unconscious forbidden wishes. Roderick's "FEAR" of total annihilation resides in his wish to be one with Madeline, to dissolve his being in the sentience of non-living matter.

Alongside my own interpretive version of Madeline, I am ready to acknowledge a grain of truth in previous interpretations of her as double or doppelgänger, or as representation of Roderick's darker consciousness, or unconscious desires, or as witch or vampire. They all miss the essential point of the perverse strategy employed in "The Fall of the House of Usher." This prose allegory is about the regulation of Desire through the fetishistic devices of Art. Roderick's aspiration for a Supernal Beauty, the pure excitement of the soul expressed in his music and painting, is the counterpoint of his bodily asceticism. By ridding himself of all earthly passion he is attempting to repudiate his incestuous longing for Madeline. However, Roderick's sublime art only disguises and conceals his forbidden wishes and in the end the Truth is out – revealed. Roderick's effort to bury the life of Desire by de-animating his still living, breathing sister is doomed to fail. Madeline's return from her walled-off place beneath the House of Usher represents the return of Usher's repudiated desires and the granting of his forbidden wishes.

The nature of Madeline's dying gesture is ambiguous. When Madeline falls inward on Roderick is it a fulfillment of their sensual passions? Or is her apparently violent gesture an act of blanketing generosity, an affirmation of their spiritual bond, a granting of her beloved brother's wish to merge with her? Either way, Madeline's final enactment represents a destruction of the symbolic order and a violation of social morality. The civil war in the palace of the mind is over. The perverse strategy has failed.

The perverse strategy employs a symbolic structure. The perverse strategy enables illusion but also still retains a connection with the moral order and reality. The price is a split-in-the-ego, much like the barely perceptible fissure that extends down the walls of the House of Usher. On the other hand, a repudiation or total denial of earthly reality entails a breakdown of symbolic structures and always invites a return of the repudiated in its most archaic and awesome guises. Whether as witch or vampire or as the specter of incestuous desire, the terrifying, emaciated, white-shrouded, bloody Madeline returns from her tomb to grant her brother's forbidden wishes. The twins are reunited in death, merged as one for all eternity. With Madeline's substantiation of the aesthetic of pure Desire, her overthrow of moral Authority, Heaven cries out, venting its full wrath on the House of Usher, which cracks apart along its fissure, collapses like a house of cards – and is no more.

NOTES

1 In *The Recognition of Edgar Allan Poe: Selected Criticism Since 1829*, ed. Eric W. Carlson (Ann Arbor: University of Michigan Press, 1966), p. 121.

2 *Collected Works of Edgar Allan Poe*, ed. Thomas Ollive Mabbott (Cambridge: Harvard University Press, 1978), vol. 3, pp. 1220–1. All further quotations of Poe's tales come from this edition; page numbers are indicated in the text.

3 Wolfgang Kayser, *The Grotesque in Art and Literature*, trans. Ulrich Weisstein (Bloomington: Indiana University Press, 1963), p. 21.

4 *Edgar Allan Poe: Essays and Reviews*, ed. G. R. Thompson (New York: The Library of America, 1984), p. 93.

5 *The Recognition of Edgar Allan Poe*, p. 277.

6 Ibid., p. 111.

7 Ibid., p. 121.

4

Detecting Truth:
The World of the Dupin Tales

DAVID VAN LEER

"Madmen are of some nation"
  −"The Murders in the Rue Morgue"[1]

WE are regularly told that Poe invented the detective story. In his groundbreaking "The Murders in the Rue Morgue" (1841), its less well known sequel "The Mystery of Marie Rogêt" (1842–43), and the trilogy's celebrated conclusion "The Purloined Letter" (1844), Poe not only wrote the first stories to achieve popularity primarily for their ingenious solutions of puzzles. He also employed many of the motifs still common in such stories – the murder in the locked room, the unjustly accused suspect, analysis by psychological deduction, and the complementary solutions of the least likely person and the most likely place. Most important, Poe created in his central character C. Auguste Dupin a model for the detective that continues to dominate mystery writing. Dupin's eccentric personality and especially his relation to his two foils – a sympathetic but naive narrator, nameless throughout the series, and an unsympathetic professional investigator, the Prefect of Police Monsieur G. – were explicitly reproduced in such detectives as Arthur Conan Doyle's Sherlock Holmes, Rex Stout's Nero Wolfe, and Agatha Christie's Hercule Poirot. Vestiges of the Dupin tales can still be seen in contemporary detective series like Robert B. Parker's novels about Spenser, Susan, and Hawk, Joseph Hansen's about Dave Brandstetter and Cecil, and Sara Paretsky's about V. I. Warshawski.

Yet the historical importance of Poe's achievement fails to tell us anything precise about either the author or the literary genre. Suspense has always been crucial in literature. In drama, Sophocles' *Oedipus Rex* and Shakespeare's *Hamlet* and *Macbeth* are especially notable for their use of techniques now primarily associated with popular detective fiction. Poe's interest in detection is not unique even among writers of prose fiction. From *Tom Jones* on, the novel has regularly treated questions about birth and inheritance as a "mystery" of origins. Before Dupin, Voltaire's *Zadig* and the Gothic tales of Ann Radcliffe, William Godwin, and E. T. A. Hoffmann explained unusual occurrences through the meticulous analysis of empirical evidence. In the decade after Poe's death, novelists Charles Dickens, Wilkie Collins, and Sheridan Le Fanu used puzzle-solving as a metaphor to critique society in Victorian England.[2]

Not only are Poe's detective devices more common than his "invention" of the genre might imply, but emphasis on his legacy to the detective tradition obscures the idiosyncrasies of the Dupin stories, those characteristics that Poe did not bequeath to his progeny. Despite their obvious interest in problem solving, the tales do not in any simple sense actually offer solutions. By withholding evidence, Poe makes second-guessing impossible. In none of the tales is the reader permitted to solve the mystery along with Dupin. Nor do the tales concern crimes in any narrowly legal sense. Only in the first is there even an identifiable murderer, who as an orangutan is neither prosecutable nor interestingly culpable. Most important, Dupin's solutions lack the moral dimension by which such fictions customarily celebrate the detective's ability to right wrongs or restructure a disordered society. These are not tales of chivalric retribution. In the first two, all misdeeds go unpunished, whereas in the third Dupin's response to the villainous but hardly illegal theft of a letter is merely to repeat the original crime in a morally ambiguous way.

If Poe invented detective fiction, detective fiction has subsequently invented him. Like many facts of literary history, Poe's interest in mystery tends to be considered apart from the philosophical and social conditions that produced it. His narrative innovations must be examined more generally for how they illumine (and obscure) Poe's intellectual universe. The important questions concern the tales' presuppositions as fully as their precursors. What kinds of beliefs would one have to have to imagine a narrative in which stories possess solutions or a world in which detection passed for knowledge? Detection in Poe is less a kind of plot than a form of truth, less a way to tell a story than a means to know the world. The real interest in these tales is not who (or what) done it but what "truth" and "world" are, how they may be reconstructed, and what follows from that construction.

1

Despite their complexity the Dupin tales are less interesting for their detective plots than for their theories about how detection works. As John Irwin remarks, the "real mystery" resides in Dupin's general problem solving ability, "that mysterious mental ability to solve a mystery."[3] Poe himself implies as much in his denial of the tales' ingenuity. Writing to his friend Philip P. Cooke in 1846, he admits,

> These tales of ratiocination owe most of their popularity to being something in a new key. I do not mean to say that they are not ingenious – but people think them more ingenious than they are – on account of their method and *air* of method. In the "Murders in the Rue Morgue," for instance, where is the ingenuity of unravelling a web which you yourself (the author) have woven for the express purpose of unravelling? The reader is made to confound the ingenuity of the supposititious Dupin with that of the writer of the story.[4]

The very structures of the tales reinforce Poe's concession that plot is of secondary importance in his depiction of the mysterious. The fractured chronology of all three narratives shifts attention from the evidence to the manner of its discovery and interpretation, and general philosophical discussions both frame the narratives and interrupt (at times overwhelm) Dupin's explication of the crimes. Even in "The Mystery of Marie Rogêt," the least philosophical of the three tales, the rehearsal of evidence is more circular than linear. The narrator's initial understanding of the basic facts of the event (724–8) is not enhanced but merely is repeated in subsequent presentations of certain newspaper accounts (729–36), Dupin's critique of these accounts (736–51), and his introduction of six additional newspaper stories, half of them not specifically concerned with the Rogêt incident (751–71). The narrative ends prematurely with a bracketed "editorial" passage assuring readers that the case was solved despite the narrative's failure to detail that solution (772).

The narrative irregularities of the series are even clearer in the two more famous tales, where general discussions of the principles of analysis occupy more of the text than do the actual crimes. "The Murders in the Rue Morgue" begins with a double introduction: first a philosophical definition of analysis, climaxing with an argument for the mental superiority of checkers and whist over chess (527–31); then a character sketch of Dupin and the narrator, ending in a bravura demonstration of Dupin's ability to predict his friend's thoughts (531–7). Even the forestalled account of the Rue Morgue murders inverts the logical order of events. A long review of newspaper commentaries (537–44) and Dupin's general musings on truth (544–8) lead to his abrupt claim to have solved the murder (548). Only the story's anticlimactic final section offers anything like an explanation of the event, largely through the sailor's account of his orangutan's murderous actions (562–8).

As French critics Lacan and Derrida have shown, "The Purloined Letter" presents an even more complexly "framed" account of a crime.[5] In this "mystery" there is never any doubt about what happened. The key actions of the story – the original theft of the Queen's letter by Minister D. and Dupin's subsequent re-theft of it – are entirely overshadowed by philosophical analysis of the situation, especially in the long discussions of the game of "even and odd," the notion of mathematical axioms, and the labeling of maps (984–90). As a result, we scarcely notice the letter's return midway through the philosophizing, and the empirical details of the various confrontation scenes are filtered through so many intermediaries – the narrator, Dupin, the Prefect, and the Queen – that we never discover the contents or even the exact appearance of the titular "letter."

The interruptions and lacunae in Dupin's explications raise questions about what constitutes truth within the tales. In most detective fiction, the detective triumphs through general keenness of observation and familiarity with recondite facts or through a more specific sensitivity to the particular psychological personalities or social environments involved. Although Dupin demonstrates some of these skills, his peculiar excellence lies in a general understanding of how the mind works. The unspoken assumption is that analytic categories organize facts rather than facts shaping knowledge. Dupin tends to conceptualize his understanding of analysis in terms of contrasting pairs – simplicity versus complexity, the profound versus the superficial, the obvious versus the abstruse, the ordinary versus the unusual. Yet the relations between these pairs are not always clear. Although his solutions aspire to simplicity, Dupin connects such simplicity with superficiality rather than profundity. Admitting that the obvious and the ordinary are equally difficult to understand, he distinguishes between the true complexity of the unusual and the false complexity of the abstruse.

Some of these contradictions may result from reading Dupin's diverse ruminations as a continuous exposition of a single philosophy, but some clarify the aspects of truth that make it detectable. Fundamentally the Dupin tales alternate between two approaches to truth. In both, truth is characterized by its self-ratifying character. Truth carries within itself its own validation. Once seen, it is immediately recognized, and anything requiring corroborating evidence from external authorities does not stand as true within Dupin's analysis. Certain that truth is always self-evident, however, Dupin describes variously the reasons for that self-confirmation. By one account truth is self-evident because it is universal. In such a context verification is deductive, moving from general principles to specific conclusions. Drawing its vocabulary from mathematical definitions of the axiomatic, verifiable truth is distinguished by its predictability.

Predictable truths are Dupin's primary domain. The reliance of his analyses on such predictability is best illustrated in the introduction to the "Rue Morgue," when Dupin apparently reads the narrator's unspoken thoughts about the inept (short) actor Chantilly. As Dupin's explanation epitomizes his analytic method, I will quote part of it at length.

"You kept your eyes upon the ground – glancing, with a petulant expression, at the holes and ruts in the pavement, (so that I saw you were still thinking of the stones,) until we reached the little alley called Lamartine, which has been paved, by way of experiment, with the overlapping and riveted blocks. Here your countenance brightened up, and, perceiving your lips move, I could not doubt that you murmured the word 'stereotomy,' a term very affectedly applied to this species of pavement. I knew that you could not say to yourself 'stereotomy' without being brought to think of atomies, and thus of the theories of Epicurus; and since, when we discussed this subject not very long ago, I mentioned to you how singularly, yet with how little notice, the vague guesses of that noble Greek had met with confirmation in the late nebular cosmogony, I felt that you could not avoid casting your eyes upward to the great *nebula* in Orion, and I certainly expected that you would do so. You did look up; and I was now assured that I had correctly followed your steps. But in that bitter *tirade* upon Chantilly, which appeared in yesterday's '*Musée,*' the satirist, making some disgraceful allusions to the cobbler's change of name upon assuming the buskin, quoted a Latin line about which we have often conversed. I mean the line

Perdidit antiquum litera prima sonum.

I told you that this was in reference to Orion, formerly written Urion; and, from certain pungencies connected with this explanation, I was aware that you could not have forgotten it. It was clear, there-fore, that you would not fail to combine the two ideas of Orion and Chantilly. That you did combine them I saw by the character of the smile which passed over your lips. You thought of the poor cobbler's immolation. So far, you had been stooping in your gait; but now I saw you draw yourself up to your full height. I was then sure that you reflected upon the diminutive figure of Chantilly. At this point I interrupted your meditations to remark that as, in fact, he *was* a very little fellow – that Chantilly – he would do better at the *Théâtre des Variétés.*'' (535–7)

Such an analytic tour de force is, as Poe himself implied in his letter, not truly ingenious. Yet it does suggest how Dupin's method deduces its conclusions from generalized concepts rather than in-ducing them from observed reality. The outside world barely in-trudes on Dupin's analysis: The narrator murmurs a word, looks up to heaven, smiles, and stops stooping. Not arising from an exact observation of details, Dupin's reasoning depends on the logical inevitability of any thought process. The narrator "could not say" a word "without being brought" to think of another word. Once thinking that second word he "could not avoid" looking upward or fail to associate the constellation he sees with yet another word. "From certain pungencies" (which Dupin forbears to enumerate) the narrator necessarily relates this Latin word to its use in a hostile review of the actor. Thought, by this account, is merely a passive and predictable combination of sensations. Though Dupin claims to have "correctly followed" his friend's thoughts, he actually anticipates them. There is nothing in the passage that counts as evidence. Most of the narrator's actions – his skyward glance, smile, and posture – corroborate what Dupin has already concluded to be the necessary train of his thoughts. Only the word "stereotomy" influences Dupin's deductions at all, and even that utterance stands not as "evidence" from which something else is inferred but merely marks the beginning of the process.

Although his solutions to the mysteries similarly assume predictability, Dupin is not entirely convinced by this universalizing approach to truth. Part of the problem is the mathematical sensibility underlying the notion of predictability. "Rue Morgue" opens by rejecting as purely mechanical the combinatory complications of chess. Near the end of "Letter," Dupin insists that logical formalism weakens all mathematical explanations. He complains:

"Mathematical axioms are *not* axioms of general truth. What is true of *relation* – of form and quantity – is often grossly false in regard to morals, for example. In this latter science it is very usually *un*true that the aggregated parts are equal to the whole.... There are numerous other mathematical truths which are only truths within the limits of *relation*. But the mathematician argues, from his *finite truths*, through habit, as if they were of an absolutely general applicability.... In short, I never yet encountered the mere mathematician who could be trusted out of equal roots, or one who did not clandestinely hold it as a point of his faith $x^2 + px$ was absolutely and unconditionally equal to q." (987–8)

Dupin's objection is twofold. First, there are situations – like morals or even chemistry – in which mathematical axioms do not apply. More important, mathematicians think that their axioms are absolute rather than situational, not "relational" but "real." There is no inside to algebra, and the only content to its notations – its "x's" and "pq's" – is that which a human mind first puts into them.

Dupin's critique of mathematical knowledge reduces the purported universality of truth to the simple observation that certain shared cultural assumptions are not currently in question. This shift from truth as unquestionable to truth as unquestioned suggests the second standard by which truth is measured in the Dupin tales – its potential for being doubted. This Cartesian definition of truth as that which cannot be doubted is historically related to and complementary to the mathematicization of knowledge. The criterion of indubitability, however, highlights different truths, even a different kind of truth, than does the criterion of universality. Unlike universal truths, indubitable ones are characterized less by their predictability than by their unpredictability. They are so unimaginable that we cannot believe them to be merely imaginary. Truth, as Dupin regularly repeats, is not profound, "not always in a well" (545). More precisely it is "by these deviations from the place of the ordinary, that reason feels its way, in its search for the true" (548; compare 736–7). Indubitability measures not the truth so unremarkable that no one yet has thought of a context in which it would not apply. It focuses on the situation so unusual (or, in Dupin's preferred term, *outré*) that no one would have imagined it had it not been so.[6]

Poe tries to bridge the gap between truth as predictable and truth as unpredictable in his concept of probability. For Dupin and the narrator, borrowing from Laplace, a "calculus of probabilities" resituates a single event, itself unpredictable, within a larger sequence of events that may be predictable.[7] Although discussions of the topic frame the narrative of "Marie Rogêt" (724, 773), Dupin's fullest explication of probability resides in his consideration of the game of "even and odd" near the end of "Letter" (983–5). Between his return of the letter and his explanation of where he found it, Dupin reviews a game in which one schoolboy dares another to predict whether his hand holds an even number of marbles or an odd. Dupin insists that the ability to predict (and therefore anticipate) the opponent's choices requires an "identification" with the other's intellect, even perhaps an ability to make one's own face "match or correspond" to his (984). This insistence is probably misguided. Not only is Dupin's theory of identification as correspondence too physiological; he may attribute too great self-consciousness to guesses made intuitively. More important, even if he rightly defines the strategies for success, Dupin does not consider that such psychological tactics are available to both players. His reading requires that only one of the boys can exploit the situation, while the other remains passive.

Perhaps Dupin's reading accurately describes the dynamics of some simple games. In even and odd the player who hides the balls may have a psychological advantage over the one who chooses. Yet a comparable depiction of one's opponents as passive mars Dupin's more complicated psychological detections. In the "Rue Morgue"'s introductory demonstration of Dupin's analytic abilities, for example, Dupin uses two mutually contradictory models to describe thought processes. Explaining how he predicted the narrator's thoughts, Dupin talks as if his own thinking were free, whereas the narrator's was determined. Dupin's associations are logical and conscious, the narrator's automatic and necessary. Such an inconsistency may merely mark Dupin's condescension to his friend's intellect. As numerous readers have noticed, however, a similar blindness informs his treatment of his intellectual equal, the malevolent but brilliant Minister D. According to the narrative's final irony, Dupin's substitution of a fake letter for the real one will eventually lead to the minister's downfall: Continuing to intimidate the Queen when he actually no longer has any power over her, D. will ultimately disgrace himself and be forced to leave the court. For his revenge to work, Dupin must assume his substitution of letters to be the final move in this game of political intrigue. Were additional moves possible, however, it would be easy to imagine other endings. The minister might, for example, discover Dupin's deception and subsequently alter his tactics, perhaps to his own advantage.

This unequal access to agency marks more than Poe's deficiencies in plotting, for in some senses detection in the tales misdescribes the ways in which truth is predictable. All accounts of the past deal with what might be called "historical necessity": the idea that something could not have not happened simply because it did in fact happen. However variously they may be interpreted, the empirical facts of the past are determinate and immutable. This historical necessity – the pastness of the past – tends in the Dupin tales to be reformulated as what might be called "teleological necessity," the idea that reasons can always be discovered to explain why something happened. These two forms of necessity are related, and most explanations of past events consider possible reasons for why things happen. Identifying contributing factors in an event, however, is not the same as saying that nothing could have been done to prevent that event. Nor would one want to deny the possibility of "the accidental," that some things just happen by chance. The tales minimize the differences between these two forms of necessity, as if describing the situation preceding an event were the same as showing what caused that event. In terms of this conflation of necessities, Dupin's tendency to deny agency to his foils marks not simply his personal ego but his philosophical confusion about what makes truth true.

2

Thus, for all their interest, Dupin's discussions of his analytic method are not entirely coherent. Throughout the tales there is a tension about the ways in which truth gets understood. In part this tension appears as differing conceptions of truth itself – universal or indubitable, complex or simple, commonplace or outré, contingent or predetermined, predictable or poetic. In part it measures incompatible vocabularies for describing truth – induction or deduction, algebra or intuition, logic or luck. In part it suggests an ambivalence about what truth can do – solve puzzles or correct injustice, prove or punish. Such tensions widen the gap in the tales between truth and detection. Although we believe both Dupin's solutions and his theories, we are never sure how closely the two relate.

These narrative discontinuities are not real, but merely mark our own tendency to misread how explanation functions in detection, to ask foolishly if Dupin's solutions are "correct." Poe reminds us in his debunking letter to Cooke that truth in fiction has a special character: It is not discovered after the fact, but created before the fact to appear as if discovered. Detection originates not in the characters' logic but in the author's, and Dupin's method is only an "*air* of method." As the opening line of "Murders" announces, "the mental features discoursed of as the analytical are, in themselves, but little susceptible of analysis" (527). The problem is not epistemological but narratological. The distinction between event and analysis required for metaanalyses is not available within a story. Any differentiation between the murders in the Rue Morgue and "The Murders in the Rue Morgue" is spurious. No narrative moment is any less fictional than any other; and within the "Murders" there is no space to be outside the "Murders." The process by which a philosophical explanation solves a mystery works more precisely to convince the reader that "a mystery" is being "solved," establishing simultaneously the literary reality of both mystery and solution. The question of how detection discovers truth becomes that of how detection constructs it – not clarifying obscurities which have, after all, been invented to be clarified, but using a fictional act of clarification to make extratextual truth possible.

The relativism of truth in the detective tales is only a specialized case of Poe's more general understanding of meaningfulness in fiction. Attacking moralistic readings of literature, Poe argues that literary truth is not a meaning but a process, residing less in homilies and morals than in a narrative consistency. Within detective fiction psychological deduction does not explain the "facts" of the crimes so much as it complements them. Dupin's analyses cannot be treated apart from the situation they explain. It is hard to imagine, for example, how one could demonstrate that on a map the names in large typefaces are *in principle* harder to see than those in small ones. Rather we should ask whether in establishing a co-dependency between theory and event detection creates a plausible literary world – whether the analysis of maps and the hiding place of the letter together draw from the "most likely place" trope an acceptable ending to the story. Such an approach to truth is called a "coherence" model: Truth is true not because it corresponds to an external reality but simply because it is internally self-consistent and hangs together ("coheres"). This coherence model of truth is in practice closely related to Poe's celebrated principle of literary construction – the "unity of effect."

The relation of unity of effect to detection, however, is ambiguous. At its simplest, unity of effect aspires to a kind of emotional consistency evident only negatively in the relatively unemotional Dupin tales. In its most complex form, the literary equivalent of Newtonian mechanics, it attributes to plot a geometric intricacy better represented by the convoluted cosmological explanations of *Eureka* than by the disjointed Dupin narratives. The special character of detection as unification may best be understood in terms of Poe's comments on the falsely didactic truth of his hated contemporary Henry Wadsworth Longfellow.

> Now with as deep a reverence for "the true" as ever inspired the bosom of mortal man, we would limit, in many respects, its modes of inculcation. We would limit to enforce them. . . . Let us then be simple and distinct. To convey "the true" we are required to dismiss from the attention all inessentials. We must be perspicuous, precise, terse. We need concentration rather than expansion of mind. We must be calm, unimpassioned, unexcited – in a word, we must be in that peculiar mood which, as nearly as possible, is the exact converse of the poetical. He must be blind indeed who cannot perceive the radical and chasmal difference between the truthful and the poetical modes of inculcation. He must be grossly wedded to conventionalisms who, in spite of this difference, shall still attempt to reconcile the obstinate oils and waters of Poetry and Truth. (CW, Vol. II, pp. 69–70)

A trial run at defining what Poe would call in "The Poetic Principle" the "heresy of *The Didactic*," this passage raises naively the distinction between truth and poetry more carefully defined in later revisions of the passage. Yet the passage recognizes that truth is "conventional" and relative, a function of its means of "inculcation." More important, it makes clear, as the revisions do not, that chief among those means is the process of simplification, of stripping away the "inessentials."

It is this process of stripping away that best defines Dupin's detection. D. A. Miller has argued that all detective fiction involves a "paradoxical economy" wherein everything might be relevant though in fact only a few things actually are. By this logic, detection never involves a "maximal integration of parts into the whole" but only the reduction of truth to "just – and no more than – what is needed to solve the crime."[8] Rather than include only such material as contributes to the desired effect, the detective tale intentionally incorporates extraneous material. The ability of the detective to separate the wheat from the chaff is what counts as detection and the effectiveness of the extraneous material is precisely its failure to contribute to the tale's final solution. The usefulness of the inessential in defining the essentialness of the true suggests how Dupin's explanations paradoxically unify through exclusion. Yet such exclusionary unification runs counter to the traditional understanding of unity of effect as total interrelationality of parts.

Thus, in one sense Poe's invention of detection seems at odds with his more general aesthetic preoccupation with unity. This contradiction may arise from the linguistic limitations of our definition of "evidence," which privileges the particulated over the whole object. As Carlo Ginzburg explains, the very notion of "clue" locates the defining characteristic of a thing in "infinitesimal traces [which] permit the comprehension of a deeper, otherwise unattainable reality." Hoofprints, stenches, and grunts count as "evidence" of a pig; the physical presence of a grunting, stinking, hoofed animal, however indisputable, does not.[9] These linguistic biases are compounded by the aesthetic requirements of the narrative within which detection takes place. Detection cannot merely explicate truth; it must surprise and entertain its readers. Whatever the tediums of real-life police work, difficulty is a prerequisite of literary detection: No easy solutions or obvious criminals need apply.

The linguistic and narrative requirements of detection suggest possible sources for some of its intellectual tensions — especially that between a truth universal and necessary and one ingenious and unexpected. They also suggest how there remain truths not representable in this form, what we might call "undetectable" truths. Most obviously, moral categories are not well suited to the narrative cleverness required of detection. In "Letter," as we saw, Dupin reads the distance between mathematics and morality to undermine the concept of the axiomatic: In morals the whole is rarely equal to the sum of its parts. The same logic can be turned against Dupin's own solutions. Neither the Ten Commandments nor the Golden Rule can be extrapolated from clues. It is traditional to argue that detective fictions posit the temporary disordering of the moral universe only to reestablish that moral order more forcefully in the identification and ostracization of the criminal. This process of recentering, however, depends on the resistance of moral precepts to the tales' mode of analysis. Detection reduces evil to a simple model of stimulus / response, accepting efficient causes as sufficient explanations of crime. The very notion of "motive" is both psychologically and morally impoverished. It asks us to believe that one murders simply for money or for revenge. The motive's motive – the sources of (and cultural encouragement for) jealousy, greed, or anger – remains unexamined, as is the paradox of why people, who should be moral, are in fact not. In this respect, the relative amorality of Dupin's detections implicitly acknowledges the deficiency of their moral vocabulary.

The inability of detection to voice moral distinctions suggests a more fundamental flaw in its description of reality. In collapsing the difference between historical and teleological necessity – between the fact that something did happen and that it had to happen – Poe employs essentially an aesthetic model of truth as self-consistency. The minimal surprise of the denouement banishes any greater surprise of narrative incoherence or irresolution. The person who actually did the deed is the person whose story best fits the established events. Even in the case of the least likely suspect – an errant orangutan – Dupin's explanations demonstrate the likelihood of the apparently unlikely through emphasizing certain narrative details – the animal brutality of the crime, the hunk of ape hair in the victim's hand. Yet such an account of truth as internally coherent undermines the very distinction between "method" and "*air* of method" on which Poe grounds his own inventiveness. In the tales, there is no difference between seeming and being. The character with the most "air of guilt" on the final page is simply declared guilty and the case closed. One wonders whether by this definition detection can ever be anything more than an air of method, and what would count as truth beyond the air of truth.

3

Detection's truth does not simply lack a moral dimension. Epistemologically self-contained, it has trouble hooking up to any external reality. With no reference point outside its own closed circuit, it even lacks a convincing standard against which to verify the distinction between the essential and the inessential on which it builds. Evaluation is hierarchical in any detective solution, but the process by which Dupin's detections "separate" the essential from the inessential becomes less a separation than an inversion: the discovery of the inessentiality of the apparently important and the essentiality of the apparently trivial. Psychologically such inversions encourage paranoia. The method of detection seems to presuppose both the hidden and the malign. Rhetorically it encourages a skillfulness tending toward sophistry, the ability to make of the lesser argument the greater. What form could separation take other than the demonstration that things are exactly the opposite of what they seem? Without an external reference how could one distinguish such a rhetoric of inversion from the suppression of the obvious?

The limitations of such rhetoric are most evident in the surprising sexual inversions of the tales. Critics have long noted that Dupin's re-theft of the letter feminizes the minister, placing him in the passive role played by the Queen in the original theft. This feminization is compounded by the Prefect's description of D. as the man "who dares all things, those unbecoming as well as those becoming a man" (976). The allusion to Macbeth's misogynist retort to his wife recalls the extent to which phrases like "acts unbecoming manhood" were in the nineteenth century usually coded references to an otherwise unnameable homosexuality. The minister is not the only figure subjected to feminization and homosexualization. Similar problems plague the depiction of the narrator's relation to Dupin. Although an erotic undercurrent informs most male-male pairings throughout both nineteenth-century American literature and the detective tradition more generally, in Poe these tensions lie especially close to the surface. In "Murders," for example, the narrator's initial illustration of Dupin's analytic technique is also an expression of his own sexual anxiety. However much the narrator's thoughts about Chantilly begin by demonstrating Dupin's detective skills, they end by distinguishing Chantilly's purported effeminacy – as represented by his superficial acting and diminutive stature – from the narrator's own embattled masculinity. If the narrator's pulling himself up to his full height tells Dupin that he is thinking of Chantilly, it should tell us that he is asserting that he is not short, that he is not gay.

The sexual oddities of detective rhetoric should redirect attention to the least familiar of the Dupin tales, "The Mystery of Marie

Rogêt." If, throughout the series, Dupin's analysis casts the criminal as female, this tale examines directly the ways in which culture reinterprets femaleness as a crime. The tale is not so successful a prose fiction as the more celebrated "Murders" or "Letter." Lacking the philosophical analyses that leaven the other tales, "Mystery" is too long, too detailed, too unshapely, and too inaccurate to offer an entertaining account of Marie Rogêt or an historical illumination of Mary Rogers from whom she derives. In attempting to solve a real-life crime, Poe faces directly in "Mystery" the intellectual paradoxes of knowing reality that he skirts around in the more conventionally successful Dupin tales. Although not entirely resolved, the dilemma of this piece displays Poe's intellectual honesty, making it a powerful meditation on, and ultimately an indictment of, the ways in which we detect truth.[10]

Poe's most obvious difficulty in solving a real-life murder involves his negotiation of the shifting relationship between reality and fiction. In his earliest drafts, the problem was primarily one of decorum: how to tell the story without violating the privacy of those still alive.[11] This problem was compounded by the newspaper publication of new evidence while the story was being serialized in the winter of 1842–43. Between the second and third installments, Poe probably made minor additions to the text to incorporate the deathbed confession of an innkeeper, who attributed Mary's death to an unsuccessful abortion conducted at her inn by an unnamed doctor. These revisions were augmented when he reprinted the story in his collected *Tales* (1845).

This final set of revisions involves more than reconciling Dupin's hypothesis about a naval officer lover with the abortion thesis. To make his explanation conform more closely to reality, Poe must recall for his readers the facts of an 1841 death largely forgotten by 1845. He adds an explanatory footnote both to insist upon his truthfulness and to review the specifics of that truth.

> On the original publication of "Marie Rogêt," the foot-notes now appended were considered unnecessary; but the lapse of several years since the tragedy upon which the tale is based, renders it expedient to give them, and also to say a few words in explanation of the general design. A young girl, *Mary Cecilia Rogers*, was mur-

dered in the vicinity of New York; and, although her death occasioned an intense and long-enduring excitement, the mystery
attending it had remained unsolved at the period when the present
paper was written and published (November, 1842). Herein, under
pretence of relating the fate of a Parisian *grisette*, the author has
followed, in minute detail, the essential, while merely paralleling
the inessential facts of the real murder of Mary Rogers. Thus all
argument founded upon the fiction is applicable to the truth; and
the investigation of the truth was the object. (723n)

Like all Poe's authorial statements, the footnote waffles between
clarification and apologetics. Even on its own terms the explanation is not convincing. The reference to "long-enduring excitement" could not but ring hollow when, only two years later, the
excitement no longer endured. Nor is Poe's interest in "the investigation of truth" a strong aesthetic defense of the tale. Not only
does it invert his customary preference for beauty over truth, it
actually diminishes the tale's value, now that the truth of Mary
Rogers is sufficiently well known to need no further investigation.
These contradictions are increased by his addition of superfluous
footnotes throughout the tale, which identify the real-life equiv-
alents of Poe's fictions. These names of forgotten people and places
do not add to the tale's reality, though the tale may add to theirs.
The inversion of fiction and fact is by 1991 complete; contemporary
readers know the historical Mary Rogers only as the model for
Poe's literary Marie.

Poe's problems keeping pace with reality result in part from the
inexorable march of time (and from his proverbial bad luck). Yet
they suggest as well the questionable principles of selection on
which detection builds and to which his footnote explicitly alludes.
Dupin's tedious analysis of "the essential" actually heightens our
interest in what falls through the cracks as "inessential." The facts
of the case are comparatively simple. Early one Sunday morning
in July of 1841 Mary Rogers left her Manhattan home telling her
fiancé Daniel Payne that she was going to visit her aunt uptown.
Her failure to return at the appointed time was distressing, but not
a cause for great alarm, as she had similarly disappeared for a few
days about three years before. When her abused body was found
three days later floating in the Hudson River south of Weehawken,

New Jersey, the police examined not only Payne but her ex-employer, cigar-store owner John Anderson, and her former boy friend Albert Crommelin. All were released without charge, and the crime attributed to wandering gangs, especially when the following September fragments of her clothes were found in the Weehawken thickets. Payne was fully absolved of the crime after his own suicide near those thickets in October. So the story rested until November 1842 (while Poe's "Mystery" was in press), when Mrs. Frederica Loss, innkeeper near Weehawken, claimed in a deathbed delirium that she and her sons had disposed of Rogers's body after an unsuccessful abortion in her inn, and that they had later planted the clothes in the thicket to deflect suspicion from themselves.

Although Dupin's solution to the mystery is flawed by his ignorance of Mrs. Loss's evidence, Poe's ordering of such material as was available is still suggestive. His disagreements with the accepted interpretation are less striking than his agreements with it. By reading against the grain, we discover in his solution less an explanation of a murder than the process by which nineteenth-century rhetoric made Mary Rogers into a mystery. Dupin attributes Marie's death (probably correctly) to the dark-complexioned man mentioned in some eyewitness accounts, who Poe thinks is Mary's officer lover, but who was more likely the nameless abortionist. Through such recourse to the least likely suspect, Poe clears of all guilt the men most closely associated with Mary – Payne, Crommelin, and Anderson.[12] In the process he isolates for criticism three elements of the newspaper accounts. Most simply he overturns the passing notion that the corpse was not Mary's. Next he undermines the argument about gang violence. Finally he exposes the late discovery of Mary's clothing as an action staged by the murderer (or his accomplices).

In all his conclusions Poe is fundamentally correct and on many of these points Dupin's detection contributes significantly to what was then understood about the case. Yet his success with the "essentials" of the murder depends on his dismissal of important details about Mary's life. Correctly challenging certain arguments that the corpse could not have been Mary's, Dupin insists that the newspapers fail to take into account the special character of what it means to be a woman. To explain why Mary was not seen early in her wanderings, Dupin argues that one must consider the general unremarkability of shopgirls on crowded city streets (749). Moreover his lengthy explanation of why Mary floated to the surface so quickly rests on the unique qualities of the specific gravity of the female body (744). These arguments for gender specificity indirectly counteract the newspapers' equally gendered reading of Mary's disappearance – that she "had absented herself from the city for reasons involving a charge against her chastity" (733). Thus Dupin's proof of the trivial truth that the corpse was Mary's entails his denial of the greater truth that her absence was related to an unwelcome pregnancy.

Similar ambiguities inform Dupin's denial of the gang theory. The journalists' desire to blame anonymous roving gangs can probably be attributed to a combination of sensationalism and xenophobia. By projecting evil onto a generalized other, this interpretation denies the possibility of middle-class crime and implicitly characterizes that other as lower-class, probably ethnic. In exposing the inapplicability of this explanation, however, Dupin reinforces the fears of class and ethnicity that generate it. The newspapers argue that the presence in the thicket of a torn piece of petticoat suggests gang activity. The use of torn cloth as a gag would only be undertaken by someone lacking a pocket handkerchief. Dupin's rejection of this argument directs itself not at the assumption that gangs are lower-class or even that the cloth was a gag. Granting these, he asserts only the class pretensions of the criminal underclass. Gang members are particularly noteworthy for their affected dress: The journalists fail to realize "how absolutely indispensable, of late years, to the thorough blackguard, has become the pocket-handkerchief" (750).

It is in light of such class and gender prejudices that we must read Dupin's defense of Payne, Crommelin, and Anderson. The innocence of all three men depends on a very narrow reading of the notion of responsibility. Payne's suicide near the site of Mary's death could easily be read as a sign of guilt rather than grief. The vagueness of his account of Mary's departure suggests that he may well have known about the intended abortion. Although Dupin peremptorily dismisses the charge, both Payne and her family were accused of suspicious apathy in response to Mary's disappearance. And, as his guilt-ridden death implies, Payne was most probably the father of the unwanted child. Though acknowledging Payne's general "suspicion" and even the "corroborative" character of his suicide, Dupin does not pursue these doubts or even challenge the newspapers' willingness to exonerate Payne (751). His notion of Mary's intended "elopement" functions, however unintentionally, to locate her fate in future activities with an unknown lover rather than in past activities with Payne.

Similarly generous is Dupin's reading of Crommelin. In trying to establish that the corpse is not Mary, one newspaper questions the reliability of Crommelin's identification of the body. Dupin is surely right to characterize the paper's insinuations against Crommelin as mere sensationalism, combined with pique at his condescension to their reporter. Yet Dupin underinterprets the significance of the hairy arm by which Crommelin identified Mary. The identification was probably based on more than the simple fact of hairiness, but Crommelin's gesture of rubbing Mary's arm to feel for hair itself demands attention. Dupin concludes that Crommelin's interest in the murder signals merely a *"romantic busybodyism"*: that he was "a suitor of Marie's; that she coquetted with him; and that he was ambitious of being thought to enjoy her fullest intimacy and confidence" (748). The perspicacity of Dupin's characterization of Mary's coquettishness and Crommelin's suit is undercut by his insistence that this sexual interest was unrealized. Crommelin's concern for the body, his acting to represent the family's interests, and especially his knowledge of what Mary's arm hair felt like in life suggest greater intimacy than Dupin acknowledges.

The contradictions in Dupin's characterization of Crommelin, simultaneously acknowledging and denying his sexualized relation to Mary, are even more striking in his treatment of Anderson. Here Poe's motive may be personal as well as intellectual; by one account Anderson himself commissioned the story to defend his reputation and reward Poe for his role in the cover-up.[13] The tale's defense of Anderson, however, if defense it is, concedes too much concerning his exploitation of his employee. Anderson plays a small but significant role in the narrator's version of the mystery.

As "Monsieur Le Blanc," he enters the account early – before Payne, Crommelin, virtually before Dupin himself – in connection with Mary's disappearance three years before, when she was still working at his cigar shop (a "perfumery" in Poe's retelling). This incident, apparently an earlier, more successful abortion, is recounted in morally ambiguous terms.

> [O]ne fine morning, after the lapse of a week, Marie, in good health, but with a somewhat saddened air, made her re-appearance at her usual counter in the perfumery. All inquiry, except that of a private character, was of course immediately hushed. Monsieur Le Blanc professed total ignorance.... Thus the affair died away, and was generally forgotten; for the girl, ostensibly to relieve herself from the impertinence of curiosity, soon bade a final adieu to the perfumer, and sought the shelter of her mother's residence in the Rue Pavée Saint Andrée. (726)

Dupin interprets the incident as a previous failed attempt at elopement. Yet Mary's "saddened air" and the inquiries of a "private character" encourage a more actively sexual reading. More important, the passage suggests Anderson's complicity in the disappearance, a suggestion that makes little sense in terms of the elopement thesis. That Le Blanc's ignorance is merely "professed" implies he actually knows something – and in fact in later years Anderson acknowledged that he had set up the first abortion.[14] Moreover the girl's subsequent retreat from the shop to the "shelter" of home may indicate flight from an "impertinence" more threatening than the curiosity that "ostensibly" caused it.

The hints of Anderson's complicity require that we reconsider his actions, less in dealing with Mary's pregnancies than in fostering the climate from which they resulted. Whatever the precise reasons that Mary left his shop, it is clear that her job there afforded her a publicity personally difficult but financially useful.

> [H]er great beauty attracted notice of a perfumer, who occupied one of the shops in the basement of the Palais Royal, and whose custom lay chiefly among the desperate adventurers infesting that neighborhood. Monsieur Le Blanc was not unaware of the advantages to be derived from the attendance of the fair Marie in his perfumery; and his liberal proposals were accepted eagerly by the girl, although with somewhat more of hesitation by Madame. (725–6)

Anderson's "liberal proposals," over which Mary's mother hesitates, may involve sex as well as employment. Whether or not Anderson's personal relation to Mary is chaste, he clearly exploits her "fair" influence on the "desperate adventurers" among district cigar smokers to increase his masculine (not to say phallic) trade. On the key point of Mary's specific duties the narrative becomes both sociologically and linguistically vague. The transition from working girl to prostitute was common enough for women in Mary's economic situation. Terms like "shopgirl" or "seamstress" were mid-century euphemisms for women whose chief source of income was their bodies.[15] It makes little difference whether Anderson literally offered Mary as a whore to his clients, or whether he just placed her in a position where assaults on her chastity would be frequent and difficult to resist. In either case, the narrative all but requires us to consider his responsibility in her downfall.

The sexual implications of Mary's position as a New York shopgirl are paradoxically heightened by Poe's relocation of the story to Paris. The move is primarily a distancing technique, allowing Dupin to treat the problem purely as a logical puzzle and protecting Poe from threat of prosecution. And, as his French enthusiasts regularly remark, the "Paris" of the tales is a fiction, with very little connection to an identifiable landscape. The fictitiousness of Poe's street names should not, however, disguise the way in which the move reinforces the sexual implications. Twice in the tale Mary is called a "*grisette,*" first in his explanatory footnote, and shortly afterward to describe how her "notorious" charms increased Anderson's trade (723, 726). The term, derived from the greyish cloth worn by the working-class woman, alludes even more explicitly than "seamstress" to the sexual habits of some workers. So overt is the implication that the word hardly counts as a euphemism. In some dictionaries the term is defined simply as "prostitute." As Felix Carlier would complain later in the century, "The *grisette* has disappeared; she has merged into the *insoumise* [kept woman]."[16]

As the move to Paris underscores the sexual dimension of the tale, so it complicates its class politics. In referring to the Prefect's desire to solve the case, the narrator associates it with his need to quell "several serious *émeutes*" (727). The term primarily refers to any form of mob action, but it recalls as well the specifically political underpinnings of riots in Paris between 1830 and 1848. The Parisian *émeutes* epitomized the generally revolutionary spirit of post-Napoleonic Europe. In associating the solution of Marie's murder with suppression of this movement, Poe recasts his "Mystery" as a proleptic *Les Misérables*, with the Prefect G. a bush-league Javert. In this politicized context, the newspapers' preoccupation with gang violence becomes not simply misguided but complicit in the Prefect's disciplinary project. Their attempts to attribute Mary's death to wandering thugs reinforce a more general attempt to discredit antiauthoritarian behavior through redefining the political "activist" as an apolitical "criminal."[17]

The conservative implications of the gang theory raise questions about the constitutive role of journalism in explaining Mary's death. Mary does not simply represent a certain culturally specific moment in the history of women's labor. As John Walsh explains, she stands as well at the dawn of a new era of sensationalism in journalism – one of its first media celebrities.[18] The appearance of a corpse in the Hudson was not a sufficiently unusual occurrence in the mid-nineteenth century for newspapers to accord it more than a few words. Yet in the case of Mary Rogers the journalists made the event into a *cause célèbre* and kept it before the public even after the police lost interest. Poe subtly suggests the newspapers' complicity in creating the mystery. The "desperate adventurers infesting the neighborhood" of the cigar store were the journalists themselves, who accounted for much of the trade at Anderson's shop in the middle of the newspaper district. Moreover, the tale's preoccupation with correcting the newspaper accounts implicitly acknowledges the degree to which the mystery existed more in the newspapers than in real life. Not only was Mary first noticed because of her potential to make good copy. The inadequacies of the explanations, which only further mystified the event, were determined by the conventions of Victorian public discourse about sexuality, the peculiar mix of prurience and prudery characteristic of yellow journalism. It might be possible to argue that in Poe a detective "style" of knowledge was always parasitic on the journalistic evidence employed to establish its "air of method." In the case of Mary Rogers, however, such an argument is much simpler: The particular cultural politics and language of mid-century journalism were necessary to turn the commonplace event of a shopgirl's abortion into a "mystery" in the first place.

"The Mystery of Marie Rogêt" is Poe's most sociologically astute tale, and his saddest – a story not of murder or theft but of the subjugation of gender and class in an early industrial urban setting. In such a history detection works not to illumine but to mystify. "The Mystery of Marie Rogêt" explores the rhetorical inversions which make invisible a socio-political reality, the process by which gender and class become "a mystery." Even as he "invents" the genre of detective fiction, Poe questions its epistemological limitations, the processes by which detection constructs truth, suppressing realities as fully as illuminating them. In light of this questioning we may want to consider our understanding of the relative successes of the Dupin tales. Current critical preference for the "Murders" or "Letter" over the "Mystery" may mark not our admiration for the intricate philosophies of the former, but our fear of the social reality in the latter.

There is an old joke about a man who, thinking *Hamlet* was a mystery, believed Fortinbras to be the true culprit, the least likely suspect who in fact inherits the kingdom in the final scene. The Dupin tales encourage us to take seriously the implications of this joke. The conventions by which we read literature always derive from clues that the texts themselves offer us. Yet those clues must be challenged even as they are accepted. In detecting truth, Dupin wishes merely to assert his authority over reality, but Poe encourages us as well to examine the undetectable truths suppressed by Dupin's detection. Until we are willing to allow that Fortinbras might be a murderer, we will have difficulty activating the national politics that *Hamlet* obscures. Only in reading against the grain of his deductions will we be able to escape Dupin's mind and enter the world that detection flees.

NOTES

1 *Collected Works of Edgar Allan Poe,* ed. Thomas Ollive Mabbott (Cambridge: Harvard University Press, 1969–), vol. 2, p. 558. Unless otherwise noted, all references to Poe's work will cite this edition in the text.

2 For classic accounts of the detective genre, see Robin W. Winks, ed., *Detective Fiction: A Collection of Critical Essays* (Woodstock, Vt.: Countryman Press, 1988). For revisions of this tradition, see John G. Cawelti, *Adventure, Mystery, and Romance: Formula Stories as Art and Popular Culture* (Chicago: University of Chicago Press, 1976); and Glenn W. Most and William W. Stowe, eds., *The Poetics of Murder: Detective Fiction and Literary Theory* (San Diego: Harcourt Brace Jovanovich, 1983). For a brilliant account of detection and surveillance in the Victorian novel, see D. A. Miller, *The Novel and the Police* (Berkeley: University of California Press, 1988).

3 John T. Irwin, "Handedness and the Self: Poe's Chess Player," *Arizona Quarterly* 45 (1989): 1.

4 *The Letters of Edgar Allan Poe,* ed. John Ward Ostrom (Cambridge: Harvard University Press, 1948), vol. 2, p. 328.

5 For the celebrated readings of Jacques Lacan and Jacques Derrida, and useful explications by Shoshana Felman and Barbara Johnson, see John P. Muller and William J. Richardson, eds., *The Purloined Poe: Lacan, Derrida and Psychoanalytic Reading* (Baltimore: Johns Hopkins University Press, 1988). For a comparable reading of Poe, that in part defines itself against the French allegories, see Stanley Cavell, *In Quest of the Ordinary: Lines of Skepticism and Romanticism* (Chicago: University of Chicago Press, 1988), pp. 105–78.

6 For a treatment of conflicting truths elsewhere in Poe, see my "'Nature's Book: The Language of Science in the American Renaissance," *Romanticism and the Sciences,* ed. Andrew Cunningham and Nicholas Jardine (Cambridge: Cambridge University Press, 1990), pp. 307–21. For a similar passage in Poe's *Eureka,* see *The Complete Works of Edgar Allan Poe,* the Virginia edition, ed. James A. Harrison (New York: Thomas Y. Crowell & Co., 1902), vol. 16, p. 228; hereafter cited as *CW* in text.

7 Concerning the double focus of probability – on statistics and epistemology, numbers and concepts – see Ian Hacking, *The Emergence of Probability: A Philosophical Study of Early Ideas About Probability, Induction and Statistical Inference* (Cambridge: Cambridge University Press, 1975), pp. 11–17. My account of probability in the following pages draws heavily on Hacking's analysis.

8 Miller, *The Novel and the Police,* pp. 33–4.

9 Carlo Ginzburg, *Clues, Myths, and the Historical Method* (Baltimore: Johns Hopkins University Press, 1989), p. 101. For discussions of the semiology of clues in terms of Peirce's theory of abduction (and Ginzburg's analysis), see Nancy Harrowitz, "The Body of the Detective

Model: Charles S. Peirce and Edgar Allan Poe," and Umberto Eco, "Horns, Hooves, Insteps: Some Hypotheses on Three Types of Abduction," both in *The Sign of Three: Dupin, Holmes, Peirce*, ed. Umberto Eco and Thomas A. Sebeok (Bloomington: Indiana University Press, 1983), pp. 179–97, 198–220. For the special place of "clues" within the Dupin tales, see John T. Irwin, "A Clew to a Clue: Locked Rooms and Labyrinths in Poe and Borges," *Raritan*, 10 (1991): 40–57.

10 For a reappraisal of this tale, see Richard P. Benton, " 'The Mystery of Marie Rogêt' – A Defense," *Studies in Short Fiction*, 6 (1969): 144–51. In praising the work, Benton reviews earlier appreciations, especially that of Dorothy L. Sayers, author of the Lord Peter Wimsey novels.

11 For the general relation between history and fiction in the story, see William Kurtz Wimsatt, Jr., "Poe and the Mystery of Mary Rogers," *PMLA*, 56 (1941): 230–48; and especially John Walsh, *Poe the Detective: The Curious Circumstances Behind* The Mystery of Marie Rogêt (New Brunswick, N.J.: Rutgers University Press, 1968); and Thomas Ollive Mabbott's notes to the standard edition (vol. 3, pp. 715–22, 774–88). My summary of the facts of the case depends entirely on the latter two critics.

12 For convenience, I shall refer to the participants by their real names rather than by Poe's pseudonyms, except where there is a significant difference in the actions of the characters and their historical prototypes. For the record, Payne is called "St. Eustache" in the tale, Crommelin "Beauvais," Anderson "Le Blanc," and Mrs. Loss "Madame LeDuc." Interestingly enough, although Loss's testimony was central in solving the murder, Poe does not identify her by name in his footnotes.

13 Walsh repeats this story but doubts its accuracy; Mabbott accepts it as plausible. See Walsh, *Poe the Detective*, pp. 81, 95; and Mabbott's headnote to the standard edition, vol. 2, pp. 720–1. At the very least one would want to recall that Anderson's involvement in the affair later prevented him from realizing his ambitions for political office.

14 See Mabbott's headnote, p. 721.

15 It is sobering, at least, to remember that "working women" is yet another euphemism for prostitutes. The literature on the overlap, both real and perceived, between working women and prostitutes is enormous. A classic early formulation is Charlotte Perkins Stetson [Gilman], *Women and Economics: A Study of the Economic Relation Between Men and Women as a Factor in Social Evolution* (Boston: Small, Maynard & Company, 1898). Among contemporary accounts see, for example,

Barbara Meil Hobson, *Uneasy Virtue: The Politics of Prostitution and the American Reform Tradition* (New York: Basic Books, Inc.,, 1987); Kathy Peiss, *Cheap Amusements: Working Women and Leisure in Turn-of-the-Century New York* (Philadelphia: Temple University Press, 1986); Ruth Rosen, *The Lost Sisterhood: Prostitution in America, 1900–1918* (Baltimore: Johns Hopkins University Press, 1982); and Christine Stansell, *City of Women: Sex and Class in New York, 1789–1860* (New York: Alfred A. Knopf, 1986). On the social status of abortion at mid-century, see James C. Mohr, *Abortion in America: The Origins and Evolution of National Policy, 1800–1900* (New York: Oxford University Press, 1978).

16 Cited in Alain Corbin, *Women for Hire: Prostitution and Sexuality in France after 1850* (Cambridge: Harvard University Press, 1990), p. 138. The usefulness of Corbin's magisterial study far exceeds its announced topic, both in its interdisciplinarity and its theoretical sophistication. See also Judith R. Walkowitz, *Prostitution and Victorian Society: Women, Class, and the State* (New York: Cambridge University Press, 1980).

17 For a fuller exploration of *"émeutes,"* see Poe's review of Frances Trollope, *Paris and the Parisians in 1835.* Here the word is coupled with a reference to Robespierre and associated with a Gavroche-like urchin shouting *"Vive la République!"* (CW, vol. 9, pp. 19–20; cf. *CW,* vol. 15, p. 10). The construction of *"the criminal"* as a depoliticizing strategy is one of the central themes in Michel Foucault, *Discipline and Punish* (New York: Pantheon, 1977). *"Mystery"* is not alone in depicting a politicized Paris. *"The Purloined Letter"* also admits of a revolutionary reading. Jacksonian Americans might not have shared the tale's desire to preserve a King's government. The story's general antirepublicanism is further complicated by Dupin's ruse for stealing back the letter. Wishing momentarily to escape observation himself, Dupin draws the Minister to the window with the sounds of a fake riot – *"the shoutings of a mob"* (992). The Minister's own position towards political unrest is unclear. We do not know if he rushes to the window in fear or support. Given Dupin's successful (and unprincipled) exploitation of revolutionary anxiety, his repeated references to the letter's *"radical"* transformation in the Minister's apartments may hint at a political subtext suppressed in the narrator's retelling (991).

18 See Walsh, *Poe the Detective,* pp. 7–8.

91

5

Poe's Art of Transformation: "The Cask of Amontillado" in Its Cultural Context

DAVID S. REYNOLDS

*/ /*T*HE Cask of Amontillado" is a prime example of Poe's ability to sculpt materials from popular literature and culture into a masterwork of terror. At once derivative and freshly individualistic, the tale enacts Poe's belief that "the truest and surest test of *originality* is the manner of handling a hackneyed subject."[1]

It has long been surmised that this story of murderous revenge reflects Poe's vindictive hatred of two prominent New York literary figures, the author Thomas Dunn English and the newspaper editor Hiram Fuller.[2] If "The Cask" is, on some level, a retaliatory document, surely Poe could not have envisioned a more ghoulish type of retaliation. Seen against the background of the war of the literati, the narrator Montresor (Poe) gets back at his enemy Fortunato (English) for a recent insult, using their mutual friend Luchesi (Fuller) as a foil in his scheme. Although we know from the start that Montresor is bent on revenge, and we have ominous feelings as he takes his foe into the depths of his skeleton-filled wine vaults, the tale's atmosphere is deceptively convivial; the two connoisseurs banter and drink as they go in search of the cask of Amontillado (a fine Spanish sherry) Montresor says he has received. Only when Montresor lures Fortunato into a small niche, quickly chains up his stupefied victim, and proceeds to wall up the niche with bricks and mortar are we overwhelmed by the horrifying fact of live burial.

Poe's animus against the literati may have motivated the revenge theme, but it fails to account for specific details of plot, character, and imagery. For those we must look to the tale's popular cultural context. Poe was a great borrower, and he had an eye on the popular market. On one level, his terror tales were clearly designed to cater to a public increasingly enamored of horror and sensationalism.[3] Writing in the era of the crime-filled penny papers and mass-produced pamphlet novels, he was well aware of the demands of the sensation-loving public. His letters are peppered with excited boasts about some work of his that has made a "sensation" or a "hit." In his tale "The Psyche Zenobia," he had the editor of a popular magazine declare: "Sensations are the great thing after all. Should you ever be drowned or hung, be sure and make a note of your sensations – they will be worth to you ten guineas a sheet" (340). Following the lead of the sensation mongers, Poe made use of some of the wildest situations imaginable.

One such situation was live burial. In "The Premature Burial" Poe wrote that "*no* event is so terribly well adapted to inspire the supremeness of bodily and of mental distress, as is burial before death," a topic that creates "a degree of appalling and intolerable horror from which the most daring imagination must recoil" (961). The specific work which established the premise of "The Cask of Amontillado" was Joel Tyler Headley's "A Man Built in a Wall," first published in the *Columbian Magazine* in 1844 and collected in Headley's *Letters from Italy* (1845).[4] Headley reports having visited an Italian church containing a niche in which was discovered the skeleton of a man who had been buried alive by a workman under the direction of the man's smirking archenemy. After a detailed description of the grotesque posture of the skeleton, suggesting an excruciatingly painful death, Headley recreates the murder:

> The workman began at the feet, and with his mortar and trowel built up with the same carelessness he would exhibit in filling any broken wall. The successful enemy stood leaning on his sword – a smile of scorn and revenge on his features – and watched the face of the man he hated, but no longer feared. . . . It was slow work fitting the pieces nicely, so as to close up the aperture with precision. . . . With care and precision the last stone was fitted in the narrow space – the trowel passed smoothly over it – a stifled groan, as if from the centre of a rock, broke the stillness – one strong shiver, and all was over. The agony had passed – revenge was satisfied, and a secret locked up for the great revelation day.

Several details in Headley's piece – the premise of live burial in a hidden niche, the careful placement of the bricks, the revenge motive, the victim's agonized groaning and numbed stillness – anticipate ''The Cask of Amontillado.''

Also analogous to Poe's story is Honoré de Balzac's ''La Grande Bretêche,'' an adaptation of which appeared in the *Democratic Review* in November 1843. Balzac describes a jealous husband who, on discovering that his wife's lover is hiding in her closet, has the closet walled up as the lady watches. Poe most likely also knew the story ''Apropos of Bores'' (*New-York Mirror,* December 2, 1837), in which a man at a party tells of going with a porter into the vast wine vaults of Lincoln's Inn to view several pipes of Madeira that were stored there. They found the pipes in good condition but had a terrifying accident: When their candle was extinguished, they groped to the cellar door only to have the key break off in the lock. They impulsively decided to forget their sorrows by staving in a wine pipe and getting drunk in order to forget ''the horrible death that awaits us.'' Giving up this impulse, they soberly faced the fact that their remains would not be discovered until all traces of identity were destroyed. We never learn the outcome of the tale, for the narrator and his listeners are called to tea before he is finished.

Another predecessor of Poe's tale, hitherto unacknowledged, was the sensational best-seller *The Quaker City; or The Monks of Monk Hall* (1845) by George Lippard, Poe's friend from his Philadelphia days.[5] Monk Hall, a huge mansion where Philadelphia's prominent citizens gather in secret revels and debauchery, has below it a so-called ''dead-vault,'' a vast cellar with labyrinthine passages and hidden recesses. The cellar is anticipatory of the vast vault beneath Montresor's mansion in several ways: It is lined with countless skeletons, its walls are clammy with moisture, and it is the scene of live burial. One critic has called ''absurd'' Poe's notion in ''Cask'' of ''an ossuary . . . gruesomely combined with the appurtenances of a wine cellar,''[6] but many of Poe's contemporary readers had been prepared for such an odd coupling by the description of Monk Hall, where not only are the wine cellar and dead-vault side-by-side but the dead-vault is littered with liquor bottles strewn amid the skeletons. In a scene that presages Montresor's long descent with his victim into the catacombs, Devil-Bug, the sadistic keeper of Monk Hall, slowly takes a victim, Luke

Harvey, down an extensive staircase into the depths of the dead-vault. Hardly as subtle as Montresor, Devil-Bug mutters to his victim, "I am a-goin' to bury you alive! D'ye hear that? I'm a-goin' to bury you alive!"[7] Just as Montresor howls and laughs at the enchained Fortunato, so Devil-Bug takes noisy pleasure in the sufferings of his victim. "He shrieked forth a horrible peal of laughter, more like the howl of a hyena, than the sound of a human laugh." Unlike Montresor, Devil-Bug does not succeed in his murderous scheme; his intended victim escapes. Devil-Bug, however, is haunted by the vision of a previous murder victim, just as (according to one reading) Montresor is tortured by the recollection of his crime.

A larger cultural phenomenon that influenced Poe was the temperance movement, which produced a body of literature and lectures filled with the kinds of horrifying images that fascinated him. Poe's bouts with the bottle, leading eventually to his death, are well known. Less familiar is Poe's ambiguous relationship with the American temperance movement. In the 1830s Poe had befriended the Baltimore writer John Lofland, who delivered temperance lectures even though, like several other backsliding reformers of the period, he drank and took drugs in private. Another of Poe's acquaintances, Timothy Shay Arthur, wrote some of the most popular (and darkest) temperance tales of the day, including *Six Nights with the Washingtonians* (1842) and *Ten Nights in a Bar-room* (1854). In the early 1840s, the rise of the Washingtonians – reformed drunkards who told grisly tales of alcoholism in an effort to frighten listeners into signing a pledge of abstinence – brought to temperance rhetoric a new sensationalism. Walt Whitman's novel *Franklin Evans* (1842), for example, written on commission for the Washingtonians, luridly depicts the ill results of alcohol, including shattered homes, infanticide, crushing poverty that leads to crime, and delirium tremens with its nightmare visions. Poe had direct association with the Washingtonians. In 1843, after a period of heavy drinking, he promised a temperance friend from whom he hoped to gain a political appointment that he would join the Washingtonians. Whether or not he did so at that time, he did join a related group, the Sons of Temperance, in the last year of his life. When on August 31, 1849, the *Banner of Temperance*

announced Poe's initiation into the order, it said: "We trust his
pen will sometimes be employed in its behalf. A vast amount of
good might be accomplished by so pungent and forcible a writer."[8]
What the *Banner of Temperance* neglected to say was that Poe
had already written temperance fiction, or more precisely, his own
version of what I would call dark temperance, a popular mode
that left didacticism behind and emphasized the perverse results
of alcoholism. Following the lead of many dark temperance writers
who portrayed once-happy families ripped asunder by a husband's
inebriety, Poe in "The Black Cat" (1843) dramatized alcohol's
ravages on an initially peaceful couple. The narrator tells us that
he had once been known for his docility and gentleness but that
his character – "through the instrumentality of the Fiend Intemperance – had (I blush to confess it) experienced a radical alteration
for the worse. I grew, day by day, more moody, more irritable,
more regardless of the feelings of others" (851). As in popular
temperance literature, the first sip is followed by escalating pathological behavior. The narrator declares that "my disease grew
upon me – for what disease is like Alcohol!" (851). One night a
"fiendish malevolence, gin-nurtured" impels him to cut out the
eye of his cat with a pen-knife, a deed he tries unsuccessfully to
drown in wine. Before long he has been driven by alcohol to
paranoia and crime, even to the extent of murdering his wife.

"The Cask of Amontillado" also studies the diseased psyche
associated with alcohol. Everything in the story revolves around
alcohol obsession. The object of the descent into the vault is a pipe
of wine. Both of the main characters are wine connoisseurs, as is
their mentioned friend Luchesi. The narrator, Montresor, boasts,
"I was skilful in the Italian vintages myself, and bought largely
whenever I could."[9] As for Fortunato, he is so vain about his
knowledge of wine and so fixated on the supposed Amontillado
that he goes willingly to his own destruction. When we meet him,
we learn "he had been drinking much" in the carnival revelry,
and as he walks unsteadily into the vault his eyes look like "two
filmy orbs that distilled the rheum of intoxication." He gets drunker
after sharing the bottle of Médoc that Montresor breaks open in
the cellar, and even more so when he subsequently gulps down
the flacon of De Grave (one of several puns that point to his fate).

97

Fortunato's name has a double meaning: from his perspective, he is "fortunate" to have an opportunity to show off his expertise in wines; from the reader's viewpoint, it is his bad "fortune" to be sucked to doom by his overriding interest in liquor.[10] Poe's contemporary readers, accustomed to dark temperance rhetoric, would have found special significance in the interweaving of alcohol and death images in passages like this:

> The wine sparkled in his eyes and the bells jingled.
> My own fancy grew warm with Medoc. We had passed through walls of piled bones, with casks and puncheons intermingling, into the inmost depths of the catacombs.

The jingling of the bells reminds us of the fool Fortunato has become because of his destructive obsession. The wine-instilled agitation of Montresor's fancy reflects his role in this devilish communion, while the intermingled casks and bones, besides recalling Lippard's Monk Hall, enhance the eerie dark temperance atmosphere. After Montresor chains Fortunato to the wall, their dialogue takes on a dreary circularity that shows once again the importance of alcohol obsession to the story. "The Amontillado!" exclaims the victim; "True, the Amontillado," replies the murderer. Even after he has been walled in, the hapless Fortunato, in a desperate attempt to pass off the situation as a joke, returns to the subject of drinking:

> "We will have many a rich laugh about it at the palazzo – he! he! he! – over our wine – he! he! he!"
> "The Amontillado!" I said.
> "He! he! he! – he! he! he! – yes, the Amontillado!"

The dark temperance mode gives the tale a grim inevitability and another cultural phenomenon – anti-Masonry – contributes to its black humor and mysterious aura. At the center of the story is a dialogue that shows Poe tapping into his contemporaries' concerns about the Masons, a private all-male order widely thought to be involved in heinous crime. After drinking the bottle of De Grave, Fortunato throws it upward with a grotesque gesture Montresor does not understand.

"You do not comprehend?" he said.

"Not I," I replied.

"Then you are not of the brotherhood."

"How?"

"You are not of the masons."

"Yes, yes," I said, "yes, yes."

"You? Impossible! A mason?"

"A mason," I replied.

"A sign," he said.

"It is this," I answered, producing a trowel from beneath the fold of my *roquelaire.*

"You jest," he exclaimed, recoiling a few paces. "But let us proceed to the Amontillado."

This marvelous moment of black humor has a range of historical associations rooted in the anti-Masonry mania that had swept America during Poe's apprentice period. The pun on "mason" (referring both to the fraternal order and to a worker in brick and stone) seems to have a specific historical referent. At the center of the Masonry controversy was one William Morgan, a brick-and-stone mason of Batavia, New York, who in 1826, after thirty years of membership in the Masons, was determined to publish a harsh exposé of the order but was silenced before he could, most likely by vindictive members of the order. Morgan's disappearance was wreathed in mystery. One night in September 1826 he was seized, gagged, and spirited away in a carriage to the Niagara frontier, where all trace of him was lost. The story spread that a group of Masons, viewing Morgan as a traitor, had drowned him in the Niagara River. (It is perhaps meaningful, in this context, that Montresor leads his victim "below the river bed.") Anti-Masonry sentiment snowballed and became a substantial political movement, peaking in the mid–1830s and then feeding into the ascendant Whig party. The Masonic order was viewed as undemocratic and as a tangible threat to American institutions. In particular, its oath, whereby members swore to uphold rational secular values (without reference to God or Christianity), was seen as sacrilegious. When Poe has Fortunato make a "grotesque" movement signaling membership in the order, he is introducing a sign that many of his readers would have regarded as demonic. When Montresor gives the sign of the trowel, he is not only foretelling the story's climax but is also summoning up the associations of brick-and-stone masonry, murderous revenge, and mysterious disappearance surrounding American Masonry.

So central is the Masonic image that the tale has been interpreted as an enactment of the historical conflict between Catholics and Masons. In this reading, Fortunato's real crime is that he is a Mason, whereas Montresor, a Roman Catholic, assumes a perverted priestly function in his ritualistic murder of his Masonic foe.[11] It should be pointed out, however, that in the predominantly evangelical Protestant America of Poe's day *both* Masons and Catholics were held suspect. If anti-Masonic feeling feeds into the portrait of Fortunato, anti-Catholic sentiment lies behind several of the grim images in the tale. In the 1830s and 1840s, American Protestant authors, fearful of the rapid growth of the Catholic church with the sudden flood of immigrants arriving from abroad, produced a large body of lurid literature aimed at exposing alleged depravity and criminality among Catholics. In 1838 one alarmed commentator wrote of the "tales of lust, and blood, and murder . . . with which the ultra-protestant is teeming."[12] Of special interest in connection with Poe's tale is Maria Monk's best-selling *Awful Disclosures of . . . the Hotel Dieu Nunnery at Montreal* (1836), which featured a huge cellar that served as both a torture chamber and a tomb, where priests had killed some 375 people and cast their remains into a lime pit. Whether or not Poe had Maria Monk and her ilk in mind when he concocted his tale of torture behind cellar walls, it is notable that he made use of Catholic images: The story is set during the *Carnivale*, a Catholic season just before Lent; Montresor's family motto about the heel crushing the serpent refers to Genesis 3:14 (the curse upon the serpent) and historically symbolizes the Church militant triumphing over the forces of evil; the early history of the Church is recalled when the underground passages are called "catacombs"; and the final words, "*In pace requiescat!*" are the last words of a requiem mass. The Catholic connection is further strengthened if we accept the idea that Poe derived the name Montresor from an old French Catholic family.[13] Although not explicitly anti-Catholic, the tale combines religious and criminal imagery in a way reminiscent of the anti-Catholic best-sellers of the day.

Though grounded in nineteenth-century American culture, ''The Cask of Amontillado'' transcends its time-specific referents because it is crafted in such a way that it remains accessible to generations of readers unfamiliar with such sources as anti-Catholicism, temperance, and live-burial literature. The special power of the tale can be understood if we take into account Poe's theories about fiction writing, developed largely in response to emerging forms of popular literature that aroused both his interest and his concern. On the one hand, as a literary professional writing for popular periodicals (''Cask'' appeared in the most popular of all, *Godey's Lady's Book*) Poe had to keep in mind the demands of an American public increasingly hungry for sensation. On the other hand, as a scrupulous craftsman he was profoundly dissatisfied with the way in which other writers handled sensational topics. John Neal's volcanic, intentionally disruptive fiction seemed energetic but formless to Poe, who saw in it ''no precision, no finish . . . – always an excessive *force* but little of refined art.''[14] Similarly, he wrote of the blackly humorous stories in Washington Irving's *Tales of a Traveller* that ''the interest is subdivided and frittered away, and their conclusions are insufficiently *climacic* [sic]'' (*ER*, 586–7). George Lippard's *The Ladye Annabel,* a dizzying novel involving medieval torture and necrophilic visions, struck him as indicative of genius yet chaotic. A serial novel by Edward Bulwer-Lytton wearied him with its ''continual and vexatious shifting of scene,'' while N. P. Willis's sensational play *Tortesa* exhibited ''the great error'' of ''*inconsequence.* Underplot is piled on underplot,'' as Willis gives us ''vast designs that terminate in nothing'' (*ER*, 153, 367).

In his own fiction Poe tried to correct the mistakes he saw in other writers. The good plot, he argued, was that from which nothing can be taken without detriment to the whole. If, as he rightly pointed out, much sensational fiction of the day was digressive and directionless, his best tales were tightly unified. Of them all, ''The Cask of Amontillado'' perhaps most clearly exemplifies the unity he aimed for.

The tale's compactness becomes instantly apparent when we

compare it with the popular live-burial works mentioned earlier. Headley's journalistic "A Man Built in a Wall" begins with a long passage about a lonely Italian inn and ends with an account of the countryside around Florence; the interpolated story about the entombed man dwells as much on the gruesome skeleton as on the vindictive crime. Balzac's "La Grande Bretêche" is a slowly developing tale in which the narrator gets mixed accounts about an old abandoned mansion near the Loire; only in the second half of the story does he learn from his landlady that the mansion had been the scene of a live burial involving a husband's jealous revenge. The entombment in "Apropos of Bores" is purely accidental (two unlucky men find themselves trapped in a wine vault) and is reduced to frivolous chatter when the narrator breaks off at the climactic moment and his listeners crack jokes and disperse to tea. Closest in spirit to Poe, perhaps, is the "dead-vault" scene in Lippard's *The Quaker City:* There is the same ritualistic descent into an immense cellar by a sadistic murderer intent on burying his victim alive. Lippard, however, constantly interrupts the scene with extraneous descriptions (he's especially fascinated by the skeletons and caskets strewn around the cellar). In addition, this is just one of countless bloodcurdling scenes in a meandering novel light-years distant, structurally, from Poe's carefully honed tale.

So tightly woven is "The Cask" that it may be seen as an effort at literary one-upsmanship on Poe's part, designed pointedly as a contrast to other, more casually constructed live-burial pieces. In his essays on popular literature, Poe expressed particular impatience with irrelevancies of plot or character. For instance, commenting on J. H. Ingraham's perfervid best-seller *Lafitte, the Pirate of the Gulf,* he wrote: "We are surfeited with unnecessary details. . . . Of outlines there are none. Not a dog yelps, unsung" (*ER,* 611).

There is absolutely no excess in "The Cask of Amontillado." Every sentence points inexorably to the horrifying climax. In the interest of achieving unity, Poe purposely leaves several questions unanswered. The tale is remarkable for what it leaves out. What are the "thousand injuries" Montresor has suffered at the hands of Fortunato? In particular, what was the "insult" that has driven Montresor to the grisly extreme of murder by live burial? What personal misfortune is he referring to when he tells his foe, "you are happy, as I once was"? Like a painter who leaves a lot of suggestive white canvas, Poe sketches character and setting lightly, excluding excess material. Even so simple a detail as the location of the action is unknown. Most assume the setting is Italy, but one commentator makes a good case for France.[15] What do we know about the main characters? As discussed, both are bibulous and proud of their connoisseurship in wines. Fortunato, besides being a Mason, is "rich, respected, admired, beloved," and there is a Lady Fortunato who will miss him. Montresor is descended from "a great and numerous family" and is wealthy enough to sustain a palazzo, servants, and extensive wine vaults.

Other than that, Poe tells very little about the two. Both exist solely to fulfill the imperatives of the plot Poe has designed. Everything Montresor does and says furthers his strategy of luring his enemy to his death. Everything Fortunato does and says reveals the fatuous extremes his vanity about wines will lead him to. Though limited, these characters are not what E. M. Forster would call flat. They swiftly come alive before our eyes because Poe describes them with acute psychological realism. Montresor is a complex Machiavellian criminal, exhibiting a full range of traits from clever ingratiation to stark sadism. Fortunato, the dupe whose pride leads to his own downfall, nevertheless exhibits enough admirable qualities that one critic has seen him as a wronged man of courtesy and good will.[16] The drama of the story lies in the carefully orchestrated interaction between the two. Poe directs our attention away from the merely sensational and toward the psychological.

Herein lies another key difference between the tale and its precursors. In none of the popular live-burial works is the *psychology* of revenge a factor. In Headley and Lippard, the victim is unconscious and thus incognizant of the murderer's designs; similarly, in Balzac there is no communication at all between the murderer and the entombed. In Poe, the relationship between the two is, to a large degree, the story. Montresor says at the start, murder is most successful if the victim is made painfully aware of what is happening: "A wrong is unredressed . . . when the avenger fails to make himself felt as such to him who has done the wrong."[17] By focusing on the process of vanity falling prey to sly revenge, Poe shifts attention to psychological subtleties ignored by the other live-burial writers.

Particularly intriguing are the brilliantly cruel ploys of Montresor. An adept in what today is called reverse psychology, Montresor never once invites Fortunato to his home or his wine vaults. Instead, he cleverly plays on his victim's vanity so that it is Fortunato who is always begging to go forward into the vaults. Montresor merely says he has received a pipe of "what passes for Amontillado," that he has his doubts, and that, since Fortunato is engaged, he is on his way to consult another connoisseur, Luchesi. By arousing vanity and introducing the element of competition ("Luchesi cannot tell Amontillado from Sherry," grumbles Fortunato[18]), Montresor never needs to push his victim toward destruction. It is the victim who does all the pushing, while the murderer repeatedly gives reasons why the journey into the cellar should be called off. This ironic role reversal begins when Fortunato, whose curiosity is piqued, demands: "Come, let us go."

> "Whither?" [asks Montresor.]
> "To your vaults."
> "My friend, no; I will not impose on your good nature. I perceive you have an engagement. Luchesi –"
> "I have no engagement; – come."
> "My friend, no. It is not the engagement, but the severe cold with which I perceive you are afflicted. The vaults are insufferably damp. They are encrusted with nitre."
> "Let us go, nevertheless. The cold is merely nothing."

And so, as Montresor tells us, "I suffered him to hurry me to my palazzo." Reverse psychology governs even Montresor's advance preparations for the murder: The palazzo is empty because he has told his servants they should not stir from the house since he would be away all night – an order "sufficient, I well knew, to insure their immediate disappearance, one and all, as soon as my back was turned." As he and Fortunato enter the vaults, he points out the white web-work of niter gleaming on the cavern walls. The mention of the niter makes Fortunato cough convulsively, at which Montresor makes a show of compassion: " 'Come,' " I said, with decision, " 'we will go back; your health is precious.' " Fortunato is resolved to go on, however, even when they pass by piles of bones. Montresor again tells him: " 'Come, we will go back ere it is too late. Your cough –,' " but Fortunato doggedly drags forward. Only when he is chained to the wall does the savage irony of the situation become clear. Montresor invites him to feel the damp niter of the wall and repeats: "Once more let me *implore* you to return. No? Then I must positively leave you. But I must first render you all the little attentions in my power." Montresor's show of concern for Fortunato is at last revealed as a craftily designed cover for murderous resolve.

There is a rigorous logic about the imagery Poe deploys in the tale. By far the most important image is the carnival. Virtually the only fact made known to us exterior to the central action or characters is that it is carnival season. When we consider the effect Poe is trying to create, we see how shrewd a choice the carnival is as a central image. To celebrate the carnival, Fortunato is dressed in motley, with a tight parti-colored costume and a conical cap and bells. His clownish dress is an apt symbol of his obtuseness as he becomes Montresor's willing dupe. The bells on his fool's cap jingle at key moments: when he first enters the catacombs; when he drinks the Médoc; and after he has been completely walled in and has given up hope. For Montresor, the carnival provides the opportunity for a perfect disguise. Before returning to his palazzo with Fortunato, Montresor dons a black silk mask and draws about him a cape, beneath which, we later learn, he has concealed a rapier and a trowel. His costume not only reflects his villainous intent but also facilitates his announced plan of murdering Fortunato with impunity: Who would know Montresor was with Fortunato the night of the latter's disappearance if both were in carnival disguise?

Yet another effect of the carnival image is to highlight, by way of contrast, Poe's terrifying climax. Fortunato's haughtiness and high spirits at the beginning of the tale bespeak a noted man of society enjoying the pleasures of the season with his wife and friends. By the end, Fortunato is in precisely the opposite of a carnival atmosphere. He faces the prospect of total isolation, degradation, and death by starvation or suffocation. Nothing could be more pathetic than his attempt to revive a carnivalesque conviviality. He calls his predicament a fine joke that will raise many a laugh over wine at the palazzo. The carnival image is now a bitter mockery of the horrid fate he confronts.

Other tokens of Poe's craftsmanship are the puns and double meanings that abound in the tale, puns that take on full significance only in retrospect, when we reach the gruesome ending. Montresor's initial greeting – "My dear Fortunato, how luckily you are met." – makes an ironic pun on Fortunato's name ("lucky") and underscores how *un*lucky Fortunato actually is. Another black joke comes when in the vault Fortunato shrugs off his bad cough: "it will not kill me. I shall not die of a cough." In light of the story's conclusion, Montresor's response is at once funny and foreboding: "True – true." It is ironic that Fortunato should raise a toast to "the buried that repose around us" (he will soon be joining them!) and equally so that Montresor replies with a toast "to your long life." A final devastating pun comes when the enchained Fortunato, in his pathetic effort to escape, says with feigned casualness, "Let us be gone." Montresor's loaded reply rings like a death knell: "Yes, let us be gone."

The double meanings surrounding the discussion of Montresor's family arms are especially telling. The arms has two contrasting meanings, dependent on perspective. The "huge human foot d'or, in a field of azure" that crushes a "serpent rampant" could stand for Fortunato, whom Montresor views as an oppressive weight to be gotten rid of; from this vantage point, the serpent's fangs embedded in the heel are symbolic of the vengeful Montresor. From a different perspective, the huge destructive foot may be said to represent Montresor's present murderous act, and the embedded fangs are the pangs of conscience he will have to live with for the rest of his life. The two perspectives illuminate different sides of Montresor's character, which is more complicated than it first appears. One side of Montresor tells him that his act of revenge is completely justified in light of the "thousand injuries" he has suffered. This side prompts his sham compassion, his wicked puns, and his sadistic behavior once Fortunato is chained up. The other side of him, which manifests itself three times toward the end of the tale, says that he himself will have to suffer as much as his victim. When the enchained Fortunato lets out a series of loud, shrill screams, Montresor recalls, "For a brief moment I hesitated

– I trembled." He then reassumes his sadistic posture, screaming even louder than his victim. Soon he pauses again, hearing the low laugh that "erected the hairs upon my head" and the "sad voice" hardly recognizable as Fortunato's. He becomes cruel again, drily repeating Fortunato's vain jokes about returning to the palazzo. But when his final call to his victim is answered only by a jingling of bells, "My heart grew sick," a confession only partly retrieved from actual compassion by the half-hearted explanation "– on account of the catacombs."

These moments when Montresor second-guesses himself have led some commentators to predict an unhappy future for him. "*In pace requiescat!*" Montresor says in conclusion, but, as Thomas O. Mabbott points out, these words may be ironic: "Fortunato had rested in peace for fifty years; Montresor must always have feared being found out" (1265–6). Does Montresor become the haunted criminal fearful of discovery, or does his callousness intensify and smother any residual feelings of remorse? Is the tale a moral exemplum on the wages of crime, or is it a gleeful portrait of a successful murder? One group of critics sees the tale as the deathbed confession of a criminal who has been tortured by guilt for fifty years.[19] According to them, Montresor's stated goal of punishing his foe with impunity is an ironic comment on the fact that Montresor himself has never been able to escape the punishment of his own conscience. In contrast, another group sees Montresor as an unrepentant, pathological killer whose crime is a source of power for him and a source of vicarious satisfaction for Poe and the reader.[20]

Is "The Cask of Amontillado" intensely moralistic or frighteningly amoral? These questions, I would say, are finally unresolvable, and their very unresolvability reflects profound paradoxes within the antebellum cultural phenomena that lie behind the tale. A fundamental feature of anti-Catholic novels, dark temperance literature, and reform novels like Lippard's *The Quaker City* is that they invariably proclaimed themselves pure and moralistic but were criticized, with justification, for being violent and perverse. Many popular American writers of Poe's day wallowed in foul moral sewers with the announced intent of scouring them clean, but their seamy texts prove that they were more interested in wallowing than in cleaning. This paradox of immoral didacticism, as I have called it elsewhere,[21] helps account for the hermeneutic circularities of "The Cask of Amontillado." On the one hand, there is evidence for a moral or even religious reading: The second sentence, "You, who know so well the nature of my soul," may be addressed to a priest to whom Montresor, now an old man, is confessing in an effort to gain deathbed expiation. On the other hand, there is no explicit moralizing, and the tale reveals an undeniable fascination with the details of cunning crime. Transforming the cultural phenomenon of immoral didacticism into a polyvalent dramatization of pathological behavior, Poe has it both ways: He satisfies the most fiendish fantasies of sensation lovers (including himself, at a time when revenge was on his mind), still retaining an aura of moral purpose. He thus serves two types of readers simultaneously: the sensationally inclined, curious about this cleverest of killers, and the religiously inclined, expectant that such a killer will eventually get his due. In the final analysis, he is pointing to the possibility that these ostensibly different kinds of readers are one and the same. Even the most devoutly religious reader, ready to grab at a moral lesson, could not help being intrigued by, and on some level moved by, this deftly told record of shrewd criminality.

Poe had famously objected to fiction that struck him as too allegorical, fiction in which imagery pointed too obviously to some exterior meaning, and had stressed that the province of literary art was not meaning but effect, not truth but pleasure. Effect is what a tale like "The Cask of Amontillado" is about. An overwhelming effect of terror is produced by this tightly knit tale that reverberates with psychological and moral implications. Curiosity and an odd kind of pleasure are stimulated by the interlocking images, by the puns and double meanings, and, surprisingly, by the ultimate humanity of the seemingly inhuman characters. Fortunato's emotional contortions as he is chained to the wall are truly frightening; they reveal depths in his character his previous cockiness had concealed. Montresor's moments of wavering suggest that Poe is delving beneath the surface of the stock revenge figure to reveal inchoate feelings of self-doubt and guilt. Unlike his many precursors in popular culture, Poe doesn't just entertain us with skeletons in the cellar. He makes us contemplate ghosts in the soul.

NOTES

1 *Collected Works of Edgar Allan Poe,* ed. Thomas Ollive Mabbott (Cambridge: Harvard University Press, 1978), p. 802. Hereafter most references to the *Collected Works* will be cited parenthetically in the text.

2 Poe's acerbic commentary on the current literary scene in "The Literati of New York City," a six-part series that ran in *Godey's Lady's Book* from May through September 1846, prompted a violent rejoinder from Fuller, editor of the *New-York Mirror* and the *New-York Evening Mirror.* When Poe's derogatory article on English appeared in the July issue of *Godey's,* English wrote a slashing reply (published in Fuller's *Evening Mirror*) which heaped insults on Poe. After additional sallies in the press, Poe filed suit for libel against English on July 23, 1846. A few weeks after the suit was filed, English's novel *1844, or the Power of the 'S.F.'* began to appear serially in Fuller's newspaper. The novel contained a satirical portrait of Poe as Marmaduke Hammerhead, a drunken, pretentious literary fop. In this bitter atmosphere "The Cask of Amontillado" was written; the tale appeared in the November issue of *Godey's.* Poe won the libel suit on February 17, 1847, and was awarded $225. See Francis P. Dedmond, " 'The Cask of Amontillado' and the War of the Literati," *Modern Language Quarterly,* 15 (1954): 137–46. A rather overstated Freudian reading of the literary battles surrounding the tale is offered in Marie Bonaparte, *The Life and Works of Edgar Allan Poe: A Psycho-Analytic Interpretation* (London: Hogarth, 1971), pp. 505–6.

3 See my discussion of popular sensational literature in *Beneath the American Renaissance: The Subversive Imagination in the Age of Emerson and Melville* (New York: Knopf, 1988), pp. 169–248.

4 The August 1844 issue of the *Columbian Magazine* in which the Headley piece appeared also contained Poe's "Mesmeric Revelation." Poe reviewed Headley's *Letters from Italy* in the August 9, 1845, issue of the *Broadway Journal.* Headley's volume was the third in Wiley and Putnam's "Library of American Books," the second being Poe's *Tales* (1845). See Joseph S. Shick, "The Origin of 'The Cask of Amontillado,' " *American Literature,* 6 (1934): 18–21. See also Mabbott's introduction to "Cask" in *Collected Works,* pp. 1253–4.

5 Poe probably met Lippard in 1842 when he was working for *Graham's Magazine*, across the street from the Philadelphia *Spirit of the Times*, where Lippard was working at the time. Lippard's satirical series "The Spermaceti Papers," published in 1843 in the Philadelphia *Citizen Soldier*, singled Poe out for praise in his generally derisive portrait of the Graham group. For his part, Poe wrote Lippard a letter on February 18, 1844, praising Lippard's novel *The Ladye Annabel* as "richly inventive and imaginative – indicative of *genius* in its author." The friendship between the writers was still strong in the summer of 1849, when Poe, penniless and hungover, struggled up to Lippard's newspaper office begging for help. Although there is no record of Poe's having read *The Quaker City*, he very likely knew of this, his friend's most significant and most popular work, which sold some sixty thousand copies in 1845, the year before Poe wrote "Cask." See *George Lippard, Prophet of Protest: Writings of an American Radical, 1822–1854*, ed. David S. Reynolds (New York: Peter Lang, 1986), pp. 256–67, and Reynolds, *George Lippard* (Boston: Twayne, 1982), pp. 8–9, 18–19, 102–10.

6 Burton R. Pollin, *Discoveries in Poe* (Notre Dame: University of Notre Dame Press, 1970), p. 29.

7 Lippard, *The Monks of Monk Hall*, ed. Leslie Fiedler (New York: Odyssey, 1970), p. 301. The next quotation in this paragraph is from p. 310.

8 *The Poe Log: A Documentary Life of Edgar Allan Poe, 1809–1849*, ed. Dwight Thomas and David K. Jackson (Boston: G. K. Hall, 1987), p. 830.

9 Quotations from the "The Cask of Amontillado" are from *Collected Works*, pp. 1252–63.

10 The connection between Fortunato and self-destructive drunkenness is further underscored by Burton Pollin's discovery that Poe may have derived this character's name from a passage about a drunken man referred to as "*Fortunate senex*" in Victor Hugo's *Notre-Dame de Paris*. See Pollin, *Discoveries in Poe*, p. 31.

11 Kathryn Montgomery Harris, "Ironic Revenge in Poe's 'The Cask of Amontillado,' " *Studies in Short Fiction*, 6 (1969):333–5.

12 David Meredith Reese, *Humbugs of New-York: Being a Remonstrance against Popular Delusion, Whether in Science, Philosophy, or Religion* (New York: John S. Taylor, 1838), p. 217.

13 See Pollin, *Discoveries in Poe*, p. 35. The Catholic connection is strengthened by yet another Montresor Poe may have been aware of: Jacques Montresor, a French officer in one of Benjamin Franklin's bagatelles

who is depicted addressing a confessor just before his death. See William H. Shurr, "Montresor's Audience in 'The Cask of Amontillado,' " *Poe Studies*, 10 (1977): 28–9. However, E. Bruce Kirkham suggests the name comes from Captain John Montresor, a wealthy British engineering officer for whom New York's Montresor's Island (now known as Randall's Island) was named. See Kirkham, "Poe's 'Cask of Amontillado' and John Montresor," *Poe Studies*, 20 (1987): 23.

14 Poe, *Essays and Reviews* (New York: Library of America, 1984), p. 1151. This volume is hereafter cited parenthetically in the text as *ER*.

15 Pollin, *Discoveries in Poe*, pp. 29–33. Pollin points out that when Poe compares Montresor's crypts with "the great catacombs of Paris" he is revealing his awareness of contemporary accounts of the great necropolis under the Faubourg St. Jacques, in which the skeletal remains of some three million former denizens of Paris were piled along the walls. One such account had appeared in the "Editor's Table" of the *Knickerbocker Magazine* for March 1838. Pollin also develops parallels between "The Cask" and Victor Hugo's *Notre-Dame de Paris*, a novel Poe knew well.

16 Joy Rea, "In Defense of Fortunato's Courtesy," *Studies in Short Fiction*, 4 (1967): 57–69. I agree, however, with William S. Doxey, who in his rebuttal to Rea emphasizes Fortunato's vanity and doltishness; see Doxey, "Concerning Fortunato's 'Courtesy,' " *Studies in Short Fiction*, 4 (1967): 266. Others have pointed out that there may be an economic motive behind the revenge scheme. Montresor, who calls the wealthy Fortunato happy "as I once was," seems to feel as though he has fallen into social insignificance and to think delusively he can regain his "fortune" by the violent destruction of his supposed nemesis, who represents his former socially prominent self. See James Gargano, " 'The Cask of Amontillado': A Masquerade of Motive and Identity," *Studies in Short Fiction*, 4 (1967): 119–26. That economic matters would be featured in this tale is not surprising, since Poe was impoverished and sickly during the period it was written. His preoccupation with money is reflected in the names Montresor, Fortunato, Luchesi ("Luchresi" in the original version) – "treasure," "fortune," and "lucre" – which, as David Ketterer points out, all add up to much the same thing (*The Rationale of Deception* [Baton Rouge: Louisiana State University Press], p. 110).

17 It is ambiguous, though, whether Montresor's stated goal is finally achieved. Jay Jacoby argues that Fortunato dies prematurely, since he is silent at the end and does not cry out in pain when Montresor's flaming torch is thrust at his head and falls at his feet. Thus the

avenger's plan of making himself known to the victim as an avenger is foiled. See Jay Jacoby, "Fortunato's Premature Demise in 'The Cask of Amontillado,' " *Poe Studies,* 12 (1979): 30–1.

18 Through this statement, Poe may be trying to show just how fatuous Fortunato is, for Amontillado is a sherry. Moreover, the fact that it is Spanish brings into question Montresor's vaunted expertise about "the Italian vintages." It is conceivable Poe himself did not know the facts about Amontillado, though one would think as a devoted drinker he would have.

19 See G. R. Thompson, *Poe's Fiction: Romantic Irony in the Gothic Tales* (Madison: University of Wisconsin Press, 1973), pp. 13–14; Thomas Pribek, "The Serpent and the Heel," *Poe Studies,* 20 (1987): 22–3; James E. Rocks, "Conflict and Motive in 'The Cask of Amontillado,' " *Poe Studies,* 5 (1972): 50–1; Kent Bales, "Poetic Justice in 'The Cask of Amontillado,' " *Poe Studies,* 5 (1972): 51; Ketterer, *The Rationale of Deception in Poe,* p. 112; J. Gerald Kennedy, *Poe, Death, and the Life of Writing* (New Haven: Yale University Press, 1987), p. 142; and Mabbott, *Collected Works,* p. 1266.

20 See Marvin Felheim, *Notes and Queries,* 199 (1954): 447–8; Vincent Buranelli, *Edgar Allan Poe* (New York: Twayne, 1961), p. 72; Edward Wagenknecht, *Edgar Allan Poe: The Man Behind the Legend* (New York: Oxford University Press, 1963), p. 161; Edward H. Davidson, *Poe: A Critical Study* (Cambridge: Harvard University Press, 1964), p. 202; Stuart Levine, *Edgar Allan Poe: Seer and Craftsman* (Deland, Florida: Everett Edwards, 1972), p. 87; Walter Stepp, "The Ironic Double in Poe's 'The Cask of Amontillado,' " *Studies in Short Fiction,* 13 (1976): 447–53; and Eric Mottram, "Law, Lawlessness, and Philosophy in Edgar Allan Poe," in *Edgar Allan Poe: The Design of Order,* ed. Robert E. Lee (London: Vision, 1987), p. 160.

21 *Beneath the American Renaissance,* Chapter 2.

6

Poe, "Ligeia," and the Problem of Dying Women

J. GERALD KENNEDY

IN "The Philosophy of Composition," that notorious essay which proclaims the death of a beautiful woman "the most poetical topic in the world," Poe devised a self-congratulatory rationale for the form and content of his popular poem, "The Raven." At the same time, however, the author also advanced a theory of aesthetics that makes pure poetry contingent on the eradication of female beauty. Through the argument that supports this judgment, Poe exposes a mechanism underlying not only "The Raven" but also several of his related poems; he indirectly comments as well on the fatalistic scheme in a handful of stories about the demise of a lovely, pale lady. Moving between verse and tale over the course of two decades, Poe persistently devised fables of loss that sent females underground, but the conditions and consequences of their erasure vary from poetry to prose in a way suggesting a conflicted response to the beautiful woman's death. In his 1845 essay, Poe distinguished between the genres in terms of their effects, calling Beauty the "sole legitimate province of the poem" and identifying Truth ("the satisfaction of the intellect") and Passion ("the excitement of the heart") as the usual objects of prose fiction.[1] In retrospect, we may infer that the author proposed this distinction partly to explain his own sharply vacillating treatment of dying women.

Through the critique of feminist theory, Poe's programmatic elimination of women has come under increasing scrutiny, and understandably so, for the pattern raises troubling questions about an inherent misogyny. Focusing mainly on the tales, recent criticism has tended to regard Poe's destructive poetics as a deliberate, ironic critique of patriarchal attitudes toward women. Seeing the narrator's final horror (in such stories as "The Fall of the House of Usher") as evidence of a failure to control or repress the female, certain commentators have even credited Poe with an enlightened deconstruction of nineteenth-century gender roles.[2] Gratifying as it may be to place Poe in the vanguard of male feminists, this political rehabilitation claims both too much and too little for his portrayal of women. A glance at the biographical evidence and a reconsideration of relevant poetry and fiction will suggest why "Ligeia" offers the definitive projection of Poe's tortured thinking about women.

1

In *The Second Sex* Simone de Beauvoir discusses, in terms remarkably apposite to Poe, the exaltation of woman in the works of André Breton. She writes that for Breton "woman is poetry," not simply its subject but the very incarnation of its essential principle: "She is Beauty above and beyond all other things" and has "no vocation other than love." Breton is drawn to this idealized woman because her beauty seems to reveal esoteric secrets and truths: "Deeply anchored in nature, very close to earth, she appears also to be the key to the beyond." Whether her name is Nadja or Mélusine, she becomes for Breton the object of an implacable quest for illumination which almost coincidentally involves sexual conquest. Through her "miraculous power," woman thus occupies a unique position as "the only possible salvation for each man." Yet this figure of adoration remains resolutely "the *other*"; although she embodies the poetic principle for the male, de Beauvoir reminds us, "we are not told whether she is poetry for herself also." In this idealization, she is paradoxically everything and nothing: "Truth, Beauty, Poetry – she is All: once more all under the form of the Other, All except herself."[3]

Apart from the sexual reference, this portrayal of woman as a beautiful, sustaining, and illuminating presence will seem entirely familiar to readers of Poe. Especially in poetry, Poe repeatedly expressed the notion that woman's love was for him the essential source of bliss, security, and life itself. In a basic sense, the individual women populating his verse all seem to incarnate the idea

114

– or ideal – of Woman. One of his earliest poems, "Al Aaraaf," evokes the image of a beloved whose beauty lies in her musicality: "Ligeia! Ligeia! / My beautiful one! / Whose harshest idea / Will to melody run." Daniel Hoffman has commented that "the chief appeal of the name 'Ligeia' to Edgarpoe was ... [that] this is the only conceivable feminine name (assuming it to be such) which rhymes with the Great Key Word, *Idea.*"[4] In "Al Aaraaf," Ligeia is indeed more an idea of musical (or poetic) creativity than a living, breathing woman; the poet writes that she has "bound many eyes / In a dreamy sleep," and implores her to arouse with "musical number" the lovely, dreaming maidens "whose sleep hath been taken / Beneath the cold moon."[5] Poe thus endows the ethereal Ligeia with a power to place women in a slumber so deep that only she can break its hold.

In more personal terms, he celebrates the nurturing, restorative power of Woman in "To Helen." The beauty of his apotheosized female brings "the weary, way-worn wanderer" home to safe harbor; her "agate lamp" is the poet's beacon, providing illumination from the "Holy-Land" of the soul. Even the inferior lyric "Eulalie" acknowledges the transformative effect of woman's love: Here, the speaker has "dwelt alone / In a world of moan" prior to his marriage; but espoused to the "radiant girl" Eulalie, he escapes all unhappiness: "Now Doubt – now Pain / Come never again." Again, in "For Annie," the poet celebrates the soothing, protective quality of woman's love:

> She tenderly kissed me,
> She fondly caressed,
> And then I fell gently
> To sleep on her breast –
> Deeply to sleep
> From the heaven of her breast.[6]

His "Annie" plays a patently maternal role, making sure that the sleeping poet is "covered" and "warm" as she prays to the "queen of the angels" for his safekeeping.

Poe openly confesses his idolatry of Woman in the late lecture "The Poetic Principle" when he explains that the (male) writer – transparently, Poe himself – finds true poetry

115

in the beauty of woman – in the grace of her step – in the lustre of her
eye – in the melody of her voice – in her soft laughter – in her sigh –
in the harmony of the rustling of her robes. He deeply feels it in her
winning endearments – in her burning enthusiasms – in her gentle
charities – in her meek and devotional endurances – but above all –
ah, far above all – he kneels to it – he worships it in the faith, in the
purity, in the strength, in the altogether divine majesty – of her *love*.[7]

This passage so obviously anticipates Breton's fetishizing of the
female as to require little elucidation. Suffice it to say that for Poe,
as for Breton, Woman holds the key not only to poetry but also
to happiness, inspiration, and productivity. For a certain kind of
male writer she is, as de Beauvoir argues, "the only possible salvation," the nurturing source of life and being who literally preserves him from death.

In many of Poe's best known poems, however, this figure of
sustenance and deliverance has already been lost, and the male
persona seeks consolation or forgetfulness as he confronts the void
of her absence. This is obviously the case in "The Raven," where
the speaker, mourning the death of the "rare and radiant" Lenore,
perversely poses to the bird just those questions which will un-
derscore his own hopelessness. The raven's "nevermore" succes-
sively rules out forgetfulness, spiritual consolation ("balm in
Gilead"), and heavenly reunion, thus foreclosing the future itself;
as the poem ends, the speaker faces an endless despair figured by
the raven's obstinate presence.

Similar abjection permeates "Ulalume" and "Annabel Lee," for
in both poems the loss of a beloved woman triggers a compulsive
return to the burial site. Composed within months of the death of
Virginia Poe, "Ulalume" suggests that astral influences have in-
duced the speaker to enter the "ghoul-haunted woodland of
Weir," where precisely a year earlier he had brought the "dread
burden" of Ulalume's body for interment. Finding his way blocked
"by the door of a tomb...the vault of [his] lost Ulalume," the
speaker suddenly perceives his unconscious reenactment of the
burial journey and asks himself: "What demon hath tempted me
here?" Reconsidering his prior interpretation of the astral signs,
he now wonders whether "merciful ghouls" have evoked the
"spectre" of the "sinfully scintillant planet" (Venus) to deflect his

movement away from the site of grief; yet his obsessive return implies an emotional desperation, a reaching out for Ulalume that betrays his own helplessness.

"Annabel Lee," on the other hand, depicts a conscious ritual of mourning. After the death of his beloved – attributed to spiteful angels – the speaker adopts the practice of lying "all the night-tide" beside Annabel's "sepulchre there by the sea" to act out the idea of his inseparability from her. Though he claims that neither angels nor demons "can ever dissever [his] soul from the soul / Of the beautiful Annabel Lee," his nocturnal routine confirms his deprivation and loss; he achieves intimacy not with his bride but with the cold tomb which signifies her irrecoverability.

In these poems, the male persona's absolute dependence on Woman's love and the bliss of female presence exposes the terrifying threat of loss (or rejection) and the withdrawal of gratification. For these pathetic figures, Woman is all, and her death generates various compulsive behaviors which imply psychic devastation. Although grief and mourning are necessary processes of accommodation to death, Poe's poems suggest that because the male protagonist has staked his entire being on the love of a beautiful woman, her absence leaves him not simply bereaved but prostrated by melancholy. He has no existence apart from the consciousness of separation from the beloved and finds his life reduced to exercises in self-inflicted anguish, indicating that the grieving male must undergo perpetual self-punishment for the unworthiness implied by the abandonment of the nurturing female.

For those familiar with the tribulations of Poe himself, this pattern has an obvious relationship to his recurrent experience of traumatic, untimely loss. Resisting autobiographical oversimplification, we may yet observe that in three notable instances, the women on whom he depended for comfort, approval, and affection – not to mention other creaturely needs – died and thus deprived him of emotional sustenance and solicitude. Poe perhaps later imagined that he himself had put the kiss of death on his mother, Elizabeth Poe, then on his foster mother, Frances Allan, and finally on his wife, Virginia Poe. When we add to this sequence the demise of the lovely and much admired Jane Stith Stanard (thought to have inspired "To Helen"), we see that Poe repeatedly suffered abandonment, or its psychic equivalent, by a dying young woman: These four ladies succumbed at an average age of thirty-one.[8]

In this context, the poet's late, curious habit of pursuing several women at once (before and after Virginia's death) betrays both an anxiety about emotional deprivation and a consuming need for female warmth and care. To Marie Louise Shew he wrote in 1848: "Unless some true and tender and pure womanly love saves me, I shall hardly last a year longer, alone." His habit of using the same terms of endearment in letters to different women reveals a conflation of emotional loyalties and even a confusion about the difference between actual, living women and an idealized notion of woman's love.[9] Increasingly enamored of female poets during Virginia's decline, Poe seems to have courted the attentions of Mrs. E. F. Ellet, Frances Sargeant Osgood, and others to solve the problem of the departing female by surrounding himself with a bevy of women who not only incarnated the poetic principle but who also wrote love poems, thus insuring a kind of affectional redundancy. At other moments he focused his complex emotional needs on his devoted mother-in-law, Maria Clemm, confessing to her: "You have been all in all to me, darling, ever beloved mother, and dearest, truest friend." After Virginia's death, he craved a new bride and fell in love with Annie Richmond, openly hoping for the decease of her husband so he could propose to her.[10] His contingency plans during those last years also included marriage proposals to the poet Sarah Helen Whitman and (just weeks before his fatal collapse) to his childhood love, Sarah Elmira Shelton. Through sheer plethora, Poe sought a loving female to protect him from desolation and death.

2

Poe's personal dependence on woman's love and his poetic evocations of the beloved's blissful presence or agonizing absence stand in contrast to the sheer malevolence in his prose versions of a beautiful woman's death. He projected in this cluster of tales an antagonism or emotional estrangement between the male protagonist and a fated female. In "The Assignation," that bizarre remnant of the early Folio Club project, a Byronic stranger saves the

Marchesa's child and thus somehow binds her to a suicide pact. "Thou hast conquered," she tells him as she prepares to poison herself an hour after sunrise. Obsessed by the wasting illness of his lovely cousin, the narrator of "Berenice" ultimately violates her tomb and disfigures her still-living body to extract the teeth which, in his diseased imagination, represent ideas. In "Morella," the narrator comes to "abhor" his wife and yearn for her death, so repelled is he by her physical dissolution; with her last breath she delivers a daughter who is the very likeness of the mother, and in a revealing gesture the narrator seems to doom the girl as well by perversely naming her Morella. A different scenario of aggression occurs in "The Fall of the House of Usher" when Roderick buries his sister Madeline alive, screwing down her coffin lid despite his worries about the "partially cataleptical character" of her illness. She avenges the act and confirms their antagonistic relationship by falling "heavily inward upon the person of her brother," bearing him to the floor "a corpse, and a victim to the terrors he had anticipated." Yet another fatal bond figures in "The Oval Portrait," which recounts an artist's compulsive portraiture of his wife, "a maiden of rarest beauty." At last the interminable sittings destroy her health and spirits, reducing her to a corpse just as the painter completes his monstrous work.[11]

Within this grouping, "Ligeia" occupies a conspicuous and revealing place. Appearing three years after "Morella," the story seemingly repeats the motif of reincarnation but with the ambiguous suggestion that the narrator's deceased first wife returns to inhabit – and transform – the body of his second wife. Just what Poe meant to represent in the final scene of metamorphosis has long provoked critical debate; in an ironic letter the author himself dismissed the view that "Ligeia [lived] again in the person of Rowena" and hinted that he should have indicated more clearly the failure of Ligeia's attempt to come back to life in the person of her successor.[12] Nevertheless, the rivalry between Ligeia and Rowena, manifested by the narrator's barely concealed scheme to debilitate his second wife, points toward a symbolic opposition thought to mirror the aesthetic differences between German and English Romanticism.[13] The implied contrast between the raven-haired, mystical Ligeia (who comes from a "decaying city by the

Rhine") and the blonde, Anglo-Saxon Rowena (named, presumably, for the heroine of Scott's *Ivanhoe*) appears to support such a reading. In the larger context of Poe's fixation with dying women, this opposition carries a more unsettling implication, though, hinting at a secret rage against women who abandon men.

Reaching back to "Al Aaraaf" for the name of his title character, Poe endowed his fictional Ligeia with harmony and musicality, for we are told that her voice creates "a melody more than mortal."[14] With the suggestion of catalepsy in Rowena's decline, he perhaps also wished to evoke the notion, implied in the poem, of Ligeia's power to impose a deathlike slumber over other women. The key point remains, however, her essentially poetic nature, which Poe underscored when, in revising the tale, he made Ligeia a poet, the putative author of "The Conqueror Worm."[15] A personification of the poetic principle, she exhibits an incomparable loveliness ("in beauty of face no maiden ever equalled her") and an indefinable expression which brings to mind transcendental analogies resembling poetic metaphors. In sum, Ligeia represents the presence of poetry within the sphere of the fictional text.

Poe emphasizes the power of that presence by recurrent references to Ligeia's enormous will – her "gigantic volition" – thus preparing us for the possibility of her return from death. He also thereby suggests her domination of the marital relationship. Possessed of "immense" learning, she instructs the narrator in arcane studies; he becomes docile and confesses: "I was sufficiently aware of her infinite supremacy to resign myself, with a child-like confidence, to her guidance through the chaotic world of metaphysical investigation" (316). Emphasizing again the juvenile character of his dependency, the narrator remarks: "Without Ligeia I was but as a child groping benighted." This simile carries more than casual significance, for if we perceive the beautiful, nurturing Ligeia as an embodiment of the *idea* of Woman in Poe's poetry, her demise thus conveys broader psychosymbolic implications.

As in "Berenice" and "Morella," the onset of Ligeia's fatal decline produces ominous physical effects: "The wild eyes blazed with a too – too glorious effulgence; the pale fingers became of the transparent, waxen hue of the grave, and the blue veins upon the lofty forehead swelled and sank impetuously with the tides of the most gentle emotion" (316). These signs of impending death sicken the narrator and evoke a "fierceness of resistance" in Ligeia, who in the very process of dying proclaims her "affection" for and "passionate devotion" to the helpless narrator. His reaction to this outpouring seems revealing, for he asks: "How had I deserved to be so blessed by such confessions? – how had I deserved to be so cursed by the removal of my beloved in the hour of her making them?" (317) His conviction that Ligeia's love for him is "all un-merited, all unworthily bestowed" reveals the narrator's own lack of ego strength and self-esteem. He is nothing; Ligeia is all. The sense that he does not merit her devotion implies his imagined worthlessness, yet he also feels indignant at his wife's "removal" just when she is showering him with affection. He seems in this mixed reaction less concerned with Ligeia's death – with the fate which *she* must undergo – than with the impending interruption of attentions necessary to his own happiness and stability.

Ligeia's struggle nevertheless comes to absorb the narrator's con-sciousness, perhaps because in an odd way, her denial of death seems an inherently masculine response to the problem of dying. Explicitly she conceives of survival as a test of volition, a bid to subjugate the body to the soul. Her reiterations of a remark at-tributed to Joseph Glanvill – that "Man doth not yield himself to the angels, nor unto death utterly, save only through the weakness of his feeble will" – testify to a fierce combativeness.[16] Annie Le-clerc has argued that the concept of masculine heroism, as reflected in modern novels and films, is precisely rooted in this notion that death must be conquered, for death amounts to the "monstrous defeat" of masculine power. Hence, according to Leclerc, men need to kill, wage wars, inflict death themselves to demonstrate their presumed mastery over mortality and to sublimate their private anxieties.[17] Ligeia's essentially masculine desire to "win in the face of death" (as Leclerc phrases it) impels her final questioning of divine will: "Shall this Conqueror be not once conquered?" Joel Porte contends that when Ligeia in "The Conqueror Worm" iden-tifies the "motley drama" as "the tragedy, 'Man,' " she thereby associates the gory Worm with "the conquering male organ."[18] Yet this reading neglects the obvious point that Ligeia is dying; she dreads death, not sexual penetration. For her, the "Horror" forming "the soul of the plot" springs from the inability of "Man" (the human species) to defeat or even to delay the predatory, "blood-red thing" which feeds upon helpless "mimes."

The dramatic emphasis of "Ligeia," however, rests less on the death of the title character than on the twisted response of a narrator "crushed into the very dust with sorrow" at the demise of his beloved. If Ligeia has articulated a fundamentally masculine resistance to the Conqueror Worm, she has in her last hours presumably voiced the narrator's deepest anxieties about death and decomposition. Given his previous "child-like" dependency, he finds himself suddenly bereft of the blissful, protective presence of his mother-mentor-wife and experiences what he explicitly calls "feelings of utter abandonment" (320). The loss of the woman who has preserved him from death triggers a psychic crisis, manifested by his "weary and aimless wandering," by his recourse to opium use, and by his obsessive renovation of a ruined English abbey. Finally, as if to avenge his abandonment by Ligeia and solve the problem of affectional deprivation, he marries the Lady Rowena "in a moment of mental alienation" (320–1). The narrator's phrase is revealing: For a moment he acts on his suppressed anger, betraying the memory of Ligeia with an impulsive remarriage.

Like those other fated ladies in Poe's fiction – Berenice, Morella, and Madeline Usher – Rowena quickly becomes an object of fear and revulsion. Unlike the poetic Ligeia, she inhabits the realm of prose, associated in "The Philosophy of Composition" not with supernal Beauty but with the expression of Truth and Passion (or "homeliness"), with realities "absolutely antagonistic" to Beauty. Insofar as she embodies the principle of prose, her very existence constitutes a reproach to the idealized memory of Ligeia. From the first Rowena arouses Passion (hatred) and the narrator's obsessive accumulation of funerary artifacts, together with his taste for grotesque and arabesque decor, implies his determination to turn the bridal bower into a torture chamber. As Roy Basler observed years ago, the narrator betrays his own deadly design by alluding to the "phantasmagoric" effect of the tapestries, an effect heightened by "the artificial introduction of a strong continual current of wind . . . giving a hideous and uneasy animation to the whole" (322). When we learn that Rowena's wasting illness has "no origin save

122

in the distemper of her fancy, or perhaps, in the phantasmagoric
influences of the chamber itself," we recognize the covert purpose
of the narrator's renovations and his cruel plan to frighten Rowena
to death.[19] In two sentences the narrator summarizes the antagonism which poisons his new marriage: "That my wife dreaded
the fierce moodiness of my temper – that she shunned me and
loved me but little – I could not help perceiving; but it gave me
rather pleasure than otherwise. I loathed her with a hatred be-
longing more to demon than to man." The second marriage has
become the obverse of the first. Love has turned to loathing and
affection to aversion. Tellingly, the narrator confesses "pleasure"
at Rowena's avoidance; perversely, he finds gratification in the
absence of intimacy.

What accounts for this immediate, unbounded hostility? According to the logic the narrator himself supplies, his contempt for
Rowena arises from his longing for Ligeia, whom he hopes to
"restore . . . to the pathway she had abandoned." As if his espousal
to Rowena has marked an emotional betrayal, he imagines that
by destroying his second wife he can somehow cancel his mistake
and effect the return of the first. The apparent metamorphosis of
the closing paragraph seems to confirm his recuperation of Ligeia,
and his undisguised yearning for her explains his seemingly gratuitous harassment of Rowena. Like the attack on the old man in
"The Tell-Tale Heart," this narrator's cruelty proves on closer in-
spection to be self-generated; it has nothing to do with Rowena's
origins, with their first month of marriage (marked by "little dis-
quietude"), or with his bride's physical appearance. In contrast to
Ligeia, who prompts an elaborate description, Rowena remains a
nonentity. Little more than a token of gender, she is yet the brunt
of a malevolent plot which begins prior to the narrator's remarriage, during the period of wandering that reveals his confusion
without Ligeia.

Even before he sets eyes on the unfortunate Rowena, he has
launched his deadly plot by purchasing the abbey and filling it
with "gorgeous and fantastic draperies" and "solemn carvings"
from Egypt – all signs of his "incipient madness." If the narrator
is intent on "alleviating [his] sorrows," then his preoccupation
with funereal artifacts displays the "child-like perversity" which

impels his actions: He will ease his grief by wallowing in death. Rather than diverting the narrator from the thought of Ligeia's death and his loss of emotional sustenance, the gloomy appointments compel him to recall that loss repeatedly, making it the defining condition of his existence. By evoking terror, the morbid decor also partakes of a scheme of symbolic retribution, for the narrator has prepared this Gothic room expressly to torment himself and the woman who would presume to replace Ligeia. The fact that he readies his chamber of horror and *then* goes looking for a bride suggests that Rowena is from the outset a sacrificial figure, a random victim of the narrator's own confused need to prove his devotion to Ligeia while avenging his abandonment by her. Contriving to unnerve Rowena, he refuses to block the "artificial" currents which stir the tapestry or even to explain to her its phantasmagoric effects as he carries out his revenge. Displacing the outrage he feels for the dead woman who has left him to languish, he projects on Rowena all his unconscious resentment of Ligeia.[20] His enmity for the second wife seems immediate and absolute because it has always been there, lodged in the unconscious, awaiting its object. If the "three or four large drops of a brilliant and ruby colored fluid" which fall into Rowena's goblet actually represent the narrator's effort to poison his wife, as Basler has argued, we witness here a confused attempt to kill two women at once: the perfidious Ligeia and her unworthy successor.

The final scenes of the tale expose the psychic ambiguity of the narrator's strategy. Simultaneously longing for his dead first wife and wishing to avenge her rejection, he watches over the "corpse" of Rowena with a "turbulent violence" of emotion, recalling "the whole of that unutterable wo [sic] with which [he] had regarded [Ligeia] thus enshrouded." Since the second "death" is a willed reenactment of the first, he gazes on Rowena's body with "a bosom full of bitter thoughts of the one only and supremely beloved" (326). Significantly, the remembrance of Ligeia's death evokes bitterness; the spectacle of the corpse awakens the memory of his *own* misery as it discloses the self-torment of his scheme. This repetition of suffering perhaps accounts for his brutal indifference to Rowena's fate. He is caught precisely between desire and disdain, between dependency and denial. Through the "hideous drama of revivification" by which Rowena appears to undergo a series of recoveries and relapses, Poe gives objective expression to the narrator's own conflicted impulses.

This conflation of the two deaths reaches its shocking conclusion when Rowena seems at last to become Ligeia. In his frenzied condition the narrator imagines that "the thing that was enshrouded advanced bodily and palpably into the middle of the apartment" (329). Here, confronted by the ambiguous image of his wildest hopes and deepest fears, he experiences a "mad disorder" of thought and perceives that the dead woman has grown taller; when the shroud falls away, the narrator sees "huge masses of long and dishevelled hair" which appears "blacker than the wings of midnight." Finally he looks into "the black, and the wild eyes" of his "lost love," Ligeia. This scene has occasioned much debate about the narrator's reliability, but the actual situation matters less than his unequivocal belief that his first wife has returned in the body of her successor. This presumed feat of metempsychosis appears to corroborate the power of Ligeia's superhuman will – as well as the pertinence of the Glanvill passage cited three times by Poe.

The narrator's conviction that Rowena has turned into Ligeia carries a deeper and more revealing import, however. Through the alchemy of that charged moment, the hated female has become the "supremely beloved" Other; the beautiful, dying woman of Poe's poetry, that source of bliss and sustenance, has merged with the despised, pale lady of the tales. The confrontation with this spectral figure dramatizes the ambiguous relations which must exist between the narrator and the woman whom he simultaneously loves and loathes. When he throws himself before her ("One bound, and I had reached her feet!"), his obeisance meets with aversion: "Shrinking from my touch, she let fall from her head the ghastly cerements which had confined it." Rowena/Ligeia responds with a gesture of avoidance linked to her own unbinding; she can only free herself from the shroud by keeping the narrator at arm's length.

In this brilliant scene fusing the two wives into a beautiful, undying woman, Poe suggests that the idolatry of the poems and the loathing of the tales are reciprocal effects of a relationship to

Woman predicated on dependency. The very instinct to idealize Woman as "All," as the incarnation of "Truth, Beauty, Poetry" and the "only possible salvation" for man, creates the basis for inevitable bitterness by making the male's happiness and self-worth contingent on sustained female affection. Within this neurotic paradigm, the absolute power of Woman (who in "Ligeia" represents beauty, learning, and will) is the inverse effect of the male's utter helplessness. By investing all value in Woman's love, the Poesque protagonist assumes a childlike subjection which, in a world of death, must result in loss and abandonment, in the withdrawal of essential gratification. The narrator of "Ligeia," of course, never suspects the connection between his adoration of Ligeia and his contempt for Rowena. Nor does he comprehend that the plot carried out in the Gothic chamber is ultimately a plot against Woman, an attack on the female loveliness he cannot live without. The pattern of violence against women throughout Poe's fiction repeatedly betrays the male protagonist's outrage at his own helplessness and insufficiency. This violence inverts the melancholy passivity of the poems and turns the experience of absence into an urge to annihilate the Other.

Only once in his later fiction did Poe represent the death of a beautiful woman as a benign event apparently uncomplicated by antagonism, resentment, or guilt. That story, "Eleonora," seems a cheerful rewriting of "Ligeia" insofar as the beloved but fated female cousin appears to sanction the narrator's subsequent marriage to Ermengarde. Read in relation to Poe's life, the story prefigures by several years his headlong quest for a new bride after Virginia's demise, offering what amounts to a prophetic argument for remarriage. Despite the narrator's vow, at the hour of Eleonora's death, that he will never "prove recreant to her dear memory" or indeed "bind [himself] in marriage to any daughter of the Earth," he later acknowledges his yearning for love and (like the narrator of "Ligeia") travels to a distant place to escape his memories of the departed one.[21] In a strange city, "bewildered and intoxicated" by the "radiant loveliness of woman," he providentially meets Ermengarde, a maiden who inspires "the most abject worship of love." This "seraph" induces a "spirit-lifting ecstasy of adoration" because her "memorial eyes" recall Eleonora. When the narrator weds Ermengarde, he imagines that the voice of Eleonora speaks to him at night, releasing him from his vow and blessing his marriage.

On the surface, this story reflects an apparent solution to the fatal dualism of "Ligeia," insofar as Poe implies a tacit collaboration between two women to fill the "void" in the narrator's heart and satisfy his longing for love. Within this happy scenario, however, lurks the perverse, childlike dependency, the pattern of relentless idolatry which – according to a psychic logic Poe had already intuited – must end in despair and anger.[22] Thus, although Poe tells a seemingly different story in "Eleonora" than in "Ligeia," we still recognize the persistent tendency of a male protagonist to grant to a beloved woman absolute control over his happiness. Whatever considerations may have prompted this ostensibly sanguine version of the death of a beautiful woman, its suggestion of an unconflicted "transferring" of the narrator's love for Eleonora to the more worldly Ermengarde ignores the mechanism of dependency-desolation-retribution depicted in "Ligeia" (and elsewhere) without supplying an equally compelling rationale for its dismantling.[23] According to the fantastic plot of "Eleonora," the dying cousin first exacts a pledge of devotion and then cancels it. In a "delirium" of passion, the narrator marries Ermengarde without a thought about "the curse [he] has invoked." Poe's final, improbable evocation of "the Spirit of Love" seems a blatant effort to invest the tale with a sentimentality which overtly mocks the concept of happy endings. As he had already demonstrated in "Ligeia," whenever the beloved Other becomes a figure of adoration, her very enshrinement makes her an object of fear and loathing, an embodiment of power ultimately despised because the male protagonist has surrendered that responsibility for his own well-being which would permit him to value a woman not as "Truth, Beauty, Poetry," but simply, humanly, as herself.

NOTES

1 "The Philosophy of Composition," *Edgar Allan Poe: Essays and Reviews,* ed. G. R. Thompson (New York: Library of America, 1984), p. 16.

127

2 This view surfaces in Leland S. Person's claim that Poe's female characters resist male efforts to transform them into "aesthetic objects," and hence that Poe implicitly criticizes these "objectifying tendencies." See *Aesthetic Headaches: Women and a Masculine Poetics in Poe, Melville, and Hawthorne* (Athens, Ga.: University of Georgia Press, 1988), p. 23. Cynthia S. Jordan presents a similar argument, though she sees a shift from the early tales (in which men repress women) to the more "androgynous," enlightened attitudes of Roderick Usher and C. Auguste Dupin. See *Second Stories: The Politics of Language, Form, and Gender in Early American Fictions* (Chapel Hill: University of North Carolina Press, 1989), pp. 133–51.

3 Simone de Beauvoir, *The Second Sex*, trans. H. M. Parshley (New York: Alfred A. Knopf, 1953), pp. 232–7. See also the similarities and differences between Poe and Breton noted by Patrizia Lombardo in *Edgar Poe et la Modernité: Breton, Barthes, Derrida, Blanchot* (Birmingham, Ala.: Summa, 1985), pp. 76–86.

4 Daniel Hoffman, *Poe Poe Poe Poe Poe Poe Poe* (Garden City, N.Y.: Doubleday, 1972), p. 247.

5 "Al Aaraaf," *Collected Works of Edgar Allan Poe*, ed. Thomas Ollive Mabbott (Cambridge: Harvard University Press, 1969), vol. 1, pp. 110–11.

6 *Collected Works of Edgar Allan Poe*, vol. 1, p. 458.

7 "The Poetic Principle," in *Edgar Allan Poe: Essays and Reviews*, ed. G. R. Thompson (New York: Library of America, 1984), pp. 93–4.

8 This figure is inflated by the relatively later death of Frances Allan at the age of forty-four; the average is based on the assumption that Elizabeth Arnold Poe was born in 1787.

9 See my discussion of Poe's letters to various women in *Poe, Death, and the Life of Writing* (New Haven: Yale University Press, 1987), pp. 101–13.

10 Letter to Maria Clemm, July 7 [1849], *The Letters of Edgar Allan Poe*, ed. John Ward Ostrom (1949; rev. ed., New York: Gordian, 1966), vol. 2, p. 452; letter to Maria Clemm, August 28–29 (?), 1849, *Letters*, vol. 2, p. 459.

11 Elsewhere I treat in slightly different terms Poe's projections of the death of the beautiful woman. See *Poe, Death, and the Life of Writing*, pp. 60–88.

12 See Poe's equivocal admission to Philip Pendleton Cooke, September 21, 1839, in *Letters*, vol 1, p. 118. There is good reason to doubt the sincerity of Poe's self-criticism.

13 This thesis appeared first in Clark Griffith, "Poe's 'Ligeia' and the

English Romantics," *University of Toronto Quarterly*, 24 (1954): 8–25. G. R. Thompson builds on Griffith's assumptions in *Poe's Fiction: Romantic Irony in the Gothic Tales* (Madison: University of Wisconsin Press, 1973), pp. 82–3.

14 "Ligeia," *Collected Works of Edgar Allan Poe*, vol. 2, p. 317. Subsequent parenthetical references to the text of "Ligeia" will correspond in pagination to this edition.

15 "The Conqueror Worm," with three sentences before and two paragraphs after the poem, was inserted when Poe revised the story for the New York *New World* in early 1845.

16 The source of this quotation has never been located, prompting speculation that perhaps Poe manufactured the esoteric allusion.

17 "Woman's Word," in *New French Feminisms*, ed. Elaine Marks and Isabelle de Courtivron (New York: Schocken, 1981), pp. 79–86.

18 *The Romance in America: Studies in Cooper, Poe, Hawthorne, Melville, and James* (Middletown, Conn.: Wesleyan University Press, 1969), p. 67.

19 See Roy P. Basler, "The Interpretation of 'Ligeia,' " in *Poe: A Collection of Critical Essays*, ed. Robert Regan (Englewood Cliffs, N.J.: Prentice-Hall, 1967), pp. 58–9.

20 It should be noted that both Leland S. Person, Jr., and Cynthia Jordan register the narrator's unconsciously repressive hostility toward Ligeia. See Person, *Aesthetic Headaches*, p. 30, and Jordan, *Second Stories*, p. 139.

21 *Collected Works of Edgar Allan Poe*, vol. 2, p. 642. Subsequent parenthetical references to the text of "Eleonora" will correspond in pagination to this edition.

22 Benjamin Fisher notes the narrator's ironic confession of madness and its ambiguous implications. See " 'Eleonora': Poe and Madness," in *Poe and His Times: The Artist and His Milieu*, ed. Benjamin Franklin Fisher IV (Baltimore: Edgar Allan Poe Society, 1990), pp. 178–88.

23 Joan Dayan has exposed the unlikeliness of Poe's conclusion to "Eleonora," calling the dead woman's supposed blessing – "Sleep in peace" – a "hollow beatitude," even a potential curse. Dayan makes another point consonant with my own argument: that Poe's transformation of woman "into superlatives, her idealization," amounts to her "reduction into generality." See *Fables of Mind: An Inquiry into Poe's Fiction* (New York: Oxford University Press, 1987), pp. 221–3.

Notes on Contributors

Christopher Benfey, Assistant Professor of English at Mount Holyoke College, is the author of *Emily Dickinson and the Problem of Others*, *Emily Dickinson: Lives of a Poet*, and *The Double Life of Stephen Crane*.

Louise J. Kaplan is a psychoanalyst practicing in New York City, and co-editor of *American Imago*. Her books include *The Family Romance of the Imposter Poet Thomas Chatterton* and *Female Perversions: The Temptations of Emma Bovary*.

J. Gerald Kennedy, Professor of English at Louisiana State University, has published *The Astonished Traveller* and *Poe, Death, and the Life of Writing*, and has completed a new book entitled *Imagining Paris: Exile, Writing, and American Identity*.

David S. Reynolds, Professor of English at the City University of New York, is the author of *Faith in Fiction: The Emergence of Religious Literature in America* and *Beneath the American Renaissance: The Subversive Imagination in the Age of Emerson and Melville* (winner of the Christian Gauss Award).

Kenneth Silverman, Professor of English at New York University, won the Pulitzer Prize in biography for *The Life and Times of Cotton Mather* and the Mystery Writers of America Edgar Award for *Edgar A. Poe: Mournful and Never-ending Remembrance*. He is currently writing a biography of Houdini.

David Van Leer, Associate Professor of English at the University of California, Davis, is the author of *Emerson's Epistemology: The Argument of the Essays.* He is now writing a study of Poe's relation to Newtonian science.

Selected Bibliography

Texts of Poe's Tales

As indicated in the various essays, all quotations from Poe's tales are drawn from the standard scholarly edition, Thomas Ollive Mabbott, ed., *Collected Works of Edgar Allan Poe*, Vols. 2 and 3 (*Tales and Sketches*) (Cambridge: Harvard University Press, 1978). Also to be recommended are Patrick F. Quinn, ed., *Edgar Allan Poe: Poetry and Tales* (New York: The Library of America, 1984) and Burton R. Pollin, ed., *Edgar Allan Poe: The Imaginary Voyages* (Boston: Twayne, 1981). These contain the texts of three lengthy tales not included in Mabbott's edition: "The Narrative of Arthur Gordon Pym," "The Unparalleled Adventure of one Hans Pfaall," and "The Journal of Julius Rodman."

Biographies and Biographical Materials

Ostrom, John Ward, ed. *The Letters of Edgar Allan Poe*. 2 vols. Rev. ed., New York: Gordian Press, 1966.

Quinn, Arthur Hobson. *Edgar Allan Poe: A Critical Biography*. New York: D. Appleton-Century, 1942.

Silverman, Kenneth. *Edgar A. Poe. Mournful and Never-ending Remembrance*. New York: HarperCollins, 1991.

Thomas, Dwight, and David K. Jackson, comps. *The Poe Log: A Documentary Life of Edgar Allan Poe 1809–1849*. Boston: G. K. Hall, 1987.

Critical Studies

Listed below are general critical studies of Poe or collections of articles about him that offer commentary on the tales featured in this volume. For additional articles on individual tales the reader should consult the footnotes to the essays in hand.

Bloom, Harold, ed. *The Tales of Poe.* New York: Chelsea House, 1987.

Carlson, Eric W., ed. *The Recognition of Edgar Allan Poe: Selected Criticism Since 1829.* Ann Arbor: University of Michigan Press, 1966.

Davidson, Edward H. *Poe: A Critical Study.* Cambridge: Harvard University Press, 1957.

Fisher, Benjamin Franklin IV, ed. *Poe at Work: Seven Textual Studies.* Baltimore: Edgar Allan Poe Society, 1978.

Hoffman, Daniel. *Poe Poe Poe Poe Poe Poe Poe.* New York: Doubleday, 1973.

Howarth, William L., ed. *Twentieth Century Interpretations of Poe's Tales: A Collection of Critical Essays.* Englewood Cliffs, N.J.: Prentice-Hall [1971].

Kennedy, J. Gerald. *Poe, Death, and the Life of Writing.* New Haven: Yale University Press, 1987.

Ketterer, David. *The Rationale of Deception in Poe.* Baton Rouge: Louisiana State University Press, 1979.

Muller, John P., and William J. Richardson, eds. *The Purloined Poe; Lacan, Derrida, and Psychoanalytic Reading.* Baltimore: Johns Hopkins University Press, 1988.

Quinn, Patrick F. *The French Face of Edgar Poe.* Carbondale: Southern Illinois University Press, 1957.

Regan, Robert, ed. *Poe: A Collection of Critical Essays.* Englewood Cliffs, N.J.: Prentice-Hall, 1967.

Thompson, G. R. *Poe's Fiction: Romantic Irony in the Gothic Tales.* Madison: University of Wisconsin Press, 1973.

Veler, Richard P., ed. *Papers on Poe: Essays in Honor of John Ward Ostrom.* Springfield, Ohio: Chantry Music Press, 1972.

Wilbur, Richard. *Responses. Prose Pieces: 1953–1976.* New York: Harcourt Brace Jovanovich [c. 1976].